T0329441

The Ways We Stretch Toward One Another

Thoughts on Anthropology through the Work of Pamela Reynolds

Edited by
Todd Meyers

Langaa Research & Publishing CIG
Mankon, Bamenda

Publisher:

Langaa RPCIG
Langaa Research & Publishing Common Initiative Group
P.O. Box 902 Mankon
Bamenda
North West Region
Cameroon
Langaagrp@gmail.com
www.langaa-rpcig.net

Distributed in and outside N. America by African Books Collective
orders@africanbookscollective.com
www.africanbookscollective.com

ISBN-10: 9956-762-71-7

ISBN-13: 978-9956-762-71-2

Table of Contents

Foreword

Francis B. Nyamnjoh

In February 2015, Langaa organised a week-long workshop in Buea on the theme of "Compulsory Retirement and the Future of Anthropology in Africa: An Intergenerational Conversation in Intellectual History." Thirty-two people (15 from Cameroon and 17 from other countries in Africa and beyond) participated in the workshop. Pamela Reynolds, whose work the current volume engages, was one of the international participants. The Wenner Gren Foundation provided some financial support for the workshop.

In the presentations, discussion and deliberations that ensued, participants scrutinised the importance of context in understanding the retirement of anthropologists in universities across the African continent. They drew on their personal experiences and on the regulations and practices in their various university institutions and countries to address such questions as the following:

- How does the retirement of anthropologists differ in different contexts?
- What are the reasons for retirement?
- What are the effects of retirement?
- What are the different ends of retirement?
- What does it really mean to be retired?
- What is the difference between being retired by a university and a personal decision to retire? Here, some felt strongly that there is no retirement as such beyond compulsory retirement. In Cameroon for example,

nobody retires as such, as compulsorily retired professors from state universities are re-employed on a contractual basis by many of the proliferating private universities. In some instances, those on retirement continue supervising students at senior level. In such instances, compulsory retirement becomes a form of circulation of resources. Whatever the prevailing situation in a given country or institutional framework, participants stressed the need to encourage anthropologists to be very professional in order not to be taken hostage by retirement.

- Is it useful to talk in terms of peaceful and painful retirements?
- Granted that, in general, universities across the continent do not seem to have planned for retirement through robust and sustained capacity building (planning and training progressively), how could those faced with compulsory retirement devise ways of outsmarting institutions who want to retire them?
- Given that retirement from university life is not always a curse, how does one cultivate positive views of such retirement through balancing, for instance, social and academic interests, time management, and the capacity to develop new forms of continued relevance?

The workshop participants partook in robust debates on the history, currency and future of anthropology in Africa as an intellectual discipline and practice, based on retirement, transmission, rupture and continuity. Questions raised and pursued included the following:

- What is the future of anthropology in the face of the reality of compulsory retirement of academic staff?
- How does the discipline address the reality of its uneven institutionalization in African universities?
- How much respect for age, wisdom, heritage (past work) is expected within different anthropological traditions? Is there reason to reread and rediscover past work in African anthropology in a more positive even if critical way? Why are classics in African anthropology classics? What lessons for why one writes and for whom?
- What has one's race or where one's umbilical cord was buried (belonging) got to do with the What, How and Why of particular approaches and processes of anthropological production and transmission? Is there room for increased conversation and accommodation between anthropology from inside out and from outside in?
- How do intellectual elders become ancestors?
- Does the younger generation of anthropologists stand to benefit from conversations with the retiring generation?
- Are there opportunities in the mass retirement of anthropologists from universities?
- What are the implications of the absence or presence of transmission of knowledge for the balance of power along lines of race, gender and generation in knowledge production?
- In what way do such conversations ensure continuity without compromising the imperative for change in the discipline?

- Granted the interest of the workshop in the production of intellectual biographies of African anthropologists and anthropologists of Africa, how do we ensure balance between their scholarly writings and their personal details?
- If it is essential to provide and account for gender dynamics in anthropological knowledge production, how should we examine the subtle and more forceful effects of gender among anthropologists and its effects in terms of knowledge production and its reception?
- How can new information and communication technologies (social media, websites, etc.) be used/mobilised to promote/facilitate intergenerational conversations with retiring and emeriti anthropologists?
- What are the interesting questions that anthropologists ask now?
- What situations have led and may lead to rethinking anthropological methods?
- Is there need for anthropology criticising and undermining truisms?

A key interest emerging before and during the workshop lay in the value of intellectual biographies based on intergenerational conversations. Participants also discussed the key indicators of an intellectual biography, stressing the need for a careful balance between personal stories and the human touch on the one hand, and the history, development and practice of their thoughts, ideas and contributions to their discipline (theoretically, methodologically, institutionally and otherwise). Participants agreed that future biographies should reflect on the extent to which the discipline of anthropology in

Africa has addressed the unfinished business of seeking reconciliation among the different intellectual traditions and histories of ethnography and anthropology in Africa and among Africans in their diversities and complexities. Here emphasis was on the colonial and postcolonial influences of particular intellectual trajectories, as well as on how ruptures in Euro-American anthropological and ethnographic traditions of knowledge had impacted Africa. Notwithstanding the positives of such ruptures, participants were more interested in establishing the extent of the deleterious effects of the ruptures in transmission (in traditions and practices of knowledge production and consumption). Equally discussed were issues such as how to acknowledge and account for ethical biases in anthropological writing, and the extent to which the dynamics of transmission were affected in contexts where anthropology had lost its disciplinary autonomy through incorporation along with other disciplines as parts of programmes. Among other things, participants felt that such joint programmes were detrimental to curriculum development and student intake. Discussions also touched on problems of epistemology. (What knowledge? How we got it, how it is organised? What is connected to what? Who is connected to whom? What are the patterns of connection that we hold dear and why?)

The most dominant theme discussed and debated at length and in detail by participants was the idea of transmission. Participants were unanimous in recognising both the imperative and responsibility to think about transmission, which is not a passive unthinking process but one that should be carefully negotiated and navigated in relation to a variety of contextual and personal factors. The socio-political context of knowledge production, circulation and transmission should be systematically factored into anthropological analyses, theory building and methodologies. The discussion centred on what it means to transmit, who gets to transmit, how to transmit and why. The following specific issues were debated at length:

- If the responsibility of an intellectual is to think, equally important is the question of what to think about.
- Is it possible to transmit what is undesirable?
- What are the problematics of the production, transmission and consumption of knowledge through research, teaching, publications and institution building?
- How does one simultaneously accommodate and resist the power of those in a position to transmit, especially in contexts of relationships between senior and junior scholars that are characterised by hierarchies of credibility?

In general, participants expressed concern that ethnographic accounts of Africa by Africans continue to be "invisible" in anthropological circles, which are still largely dominated by anthropologists, publishers and journals situated mainly in the global north. African intellectuals have not often been in a position to write on equal terms with non-Africans within the dominant colonial, postcolonial, and neoliberal political economy of knowledge production. Much intellectual work of anthropological relevance in Africa is often produced in relations of inequality, necessitating widespread participation in consultancy work. This makes of consultancy reports and kindred literature a potential rich source of information on how many an African anthropologist and fellow social scientists insert anthropological and related insights into texts that are often produced under conditions of intellectual contestation about the status and rationality of local knowledge and the right to resources.

At the end of the workshop, participants agreed on two key preoccupations, namely: (i) Given their limited access to international journals and publishers, what alternative channels do African anthropologists avail themselves with for the research they do? (ii) How can the idea of transmission through intergenerational conversations be taken forward? Participants agreed on two models (i) pursue the idea of an edited volume based on a study of consultancy reports produced by African anthropologists, to establish the extent to which parallel channels of generating and disseminating anthropological knowledge exist and operate in and among Africans, that may or may not be visible to dominant conventional scholarly channels and avenues; and (ii) ensure transmission through continued intergenerational conversations. The workshop concluded with the launch of an Intellectual Biography Series in African Anthropology with Langaa Research and Publishing in Cameroon.

The Ways We Stretch Toward One Another is the first volume in the series. In addition to an interview on how anthropologists are fashioned and fashion, the book is comprised of essays by five scholars in different stages of their academic careers, written in active conversation with Pamela Reynolds, her thoughts and works. The authors share an intimate intellectual knowledge of and engagement with Reynolds and her contribution to anthropology in Africa and globally. In the spirit of intergenerational interconnections and interdependencies, these essays are testament to the infinite spectrum of possibilities available for disciplinary renewal through well-negotiated and carefully navigated forms and modes of transmission.

Editor's Note

Todd Meyers

It astonishes how difficult it is to truly identify influence. Sure, there are moments in art and literature when the rhyming between two creations independently produced can be said to work "from" and "off" one another. We hear music that shares tempos or refrains that reminds us of something we have heard before; whole genres and traditions are carried into others. Things are borrowed, taken up, passed down, paid homage, and, sometimes, become the object of theft. But influence is greater than the identification of commonality, of something fixed in the properties of a work. John Milton influenced Ernest Hemingway, though good luck finding those passages where the younger man finds his voice through the older. It is hard to name a hip-hop artist who does not claim Thelonious Monk or John Coltrane as part of an intimate musical genealogy. And, often, in art and music and anthropology, such forms of influence come with hefty doses of matricide or patricide. There are passive forms of influence that are either pulled from a collective history or owed to a reappraisal of one's own route after arriving at some destination.

Yet this volume is concerned with (for lack of a better term) a *haptic* form of influence, from the touch of the one doing the influencing. Knowing this form of influence requires us (failingly) to trace something back to a moment of departure, to recognize how we were nudged or redirected, perhaps imperceptibly at the time, but years after sailing from port, those tiny degrees of adjustment sent us on courses miles and miles from where we may have otherwise travelled.

The following essays give varied expression to the problems and joys of influence, of legacy and debt. The essays are written by a small group of scholars who learned with and from Pamela Reynolds, each at different points in scholarly careers, each at a different place in an occupation in and around anthropology. Together the essays, I suppose, form a *festschrift*, but the spirit of the contributions seems to me something greater than solely honouring a senior scholar—or rather, each author finds a different route from and through Pamela and her work, moving outward into the world, stretching toward anthropological domains and different worlds of encounter with help from Pamela. Inheritance (with all the baggage this carries), debts of various magnitudes (each equally unpayable), shared intellectual and political stakes, guidance and care— these are the themes that dance on the surface of an older, deeper question about learning anthropology, and tangling with what anthropology is and can mean. As the editor, I deem the volume an utter failure if its purpose is mistaken for simple gratitude or, worse, to add some kind of punctuation to Pamela Reynolds' lengthy career. We should be so lucky as to have Pamela upend our essays altogether, to tell us to stop concerning ourselves with her and to get back to our own work! Not for reasons of embarrassment or false humility, but because Pamela Reynolds has demonstrated for each of us, in her own way, a sensibility that keeps pride in check and inspires us to work, often on questions and in circumstances that resist work and thought.

It should be said that this collection contains only a tiny handful of those who have encountered and benefited from knowing the person and her work. But if influence is hard to locate, it is even harder to attach thankfulness to this moving target. Maybe this is the movement of anthropology. Maybe this is the action of learning together.

*****

I would like to thank Pamela and Francis Nyamnjoh for the opportunity to work with them on *The Ways We Stretch Toward One Another*, and to the contributors for taking on the unsurprisingly difficult and rewarding task of writing about Pamela and her work. Elizabeth Goodenough's students, Sophia Georginis, Susan LaMoreaux, and Alyssa Erebor, generously organized the interview with Pamela and allowed us to reproduce it here. The cover photograph is of Pamela and her co-worker, Anderson Mangisi, in Omay, Zambezi Valley in 1984, as they write in the shade of "Manhattan," Pamela's busanza, with children watching. We are grateful to reproduce it here. Many thanks go to the editors at Langaa Research and Publishing Common Initiative Group for making the volume possible.

Index Card, Injunctions and Independence:
Thoughts on relationship

Fiona C. Ross

"Do with them as you will".

This was the final sentence on an index card at the end of Pamela Reynolds' first comments on draft chapters of my Ph.D., more than a decade and a half ago. A gift. A command. An injunction. As such, the words are impossible to live up to and simultaneously impossible to deny.

Pamela's comments on my work had offered a generous insight and careful critique of my ideas about the workings and effects of South Africa's Truth and Reconciliation Commission. As a young graduate student involved in a fraught and complex research project on political activism, trauma and truth-telling in South Africa, I was inclined to take them at face-value and to simply adjust my thought to hers. Perhaps I did so to some extent. But the injunction "Do with them as you will" offered pause. I read it as asking me to take responsibility for my own thought under the guidance of hers; to make decisions that might or might not accord with her thought; to live up to what was afforded in the generosity of intellectual relationship.

It is sixteen years since I was Pamela's graduate student, and fully two decades since I began working with her, first as a research assistant, then a graduate student, then as colleague and friend. We have not collaborated on another project together, although there are lineaments of connection between her life's work and the spaces of thought I now inhabit. Her index card's injunction has remained a shaping force for me all these years.

The phrase, "Do with them as you will" and my receipt of it, have suggested the questions I pose below. They seem particularly apposite not only in the singularity of our relationship, but more broadly in relation to events in contemporary South Africa (where epistemologies, methods and practices are under serious scrutiny from lively young scholars, impatient with the South African academy's recalcitrance to change). What does it mean to enter a tutelage relationship? To seek mentorship and be granted it? Who can predict the effects, shaping and longevities of our relationships, their consequences? Who can know what may come of them; in what forms they might enter a life, take root, take life, be uprooted? How do others shape us? What do we inherit? What can we reshape? To what are we responsive? Resistant? Why? What slips us by? How do we know? What tools, techniques, potentials, limits do our relationships offer? What might we take of what is afforded to use and what should we leave? How do we make futures with what is available at hand? How do our models of the world do us injustice?

I cannot answer all of these questions here and indeed would be wary of the attempt to fix responses; the questions and the thoughts they provoke shift over time and in response to different stimuli. It is very hard to untangle in the moment the ways that we are shaped by others over time. It has not been easy to write of our relationship here; that luxury—as with her own comments on Monica Wilson[1]—is

2

usually afforded much later in life, when, as Veena Das has so persuasively described, time has done its work in rendering the lineaments of responsibility and one's place in the collective clear. [2] One cannot know except through interpretation and with hindsight. I see the questions I've posed rather as an affordance, as a way to think about relationships and effects. The paper is an attempt to grapple with this through close attention to Pamela's extraordinary corpus of work. If I do not offer much of myself, it is out of respect and with the knowledge that my thought is itself shaped by our relationship.

*****

Pamela Reynolds' corpus of work on childhoods in Southern Africa is extraordinary. She has written accounts of childhood and youth, of the place of the family and elders, of the formation of culture and its transmission, and of the effects of violence on the constitution of relationships and the self. It reframed philosophical questions as questions of culture and practice; matters about which anthropological questions might be posed and ethnographic answers sought. Her work draws from multiple sources: literature, philosophy, ethnography. It is shaped by a deep commitment to observing and recording what is there. Her attentiveness is shaped by methodological rigour and a commitment to the production of data. I concentrate on these while exploring the entailments of her thought.

Reynolds' seminal account of childhood, *Childhood in Crossroads*, begins with the understated observation that "No serious attempts have been made to write an ethnography using children as informants or to study cognitive

3

development in the full context of living and growing in South Africa." [3] The book is an account of the lives of children aged seven at the beginning of research, who were living in Crossroads, Cape Town, South Africa, in the late 1970s and early 1980s. It was the height of apartheid, and a time of terrible state violence against Africans. The argument of *Childhood in Crossroads* is broad. Using Piaget's work on children's cognitive development, it seeks to explore children's thought, and thence their worlds by probing their ideas on different topics – kinship, song, play, dreams, order "from different angles and across time." [4] As has become characteristic of her work, Reynolds draws on philosophy and other disciplines in the making of a properly anthropological account. She is unafraid to experiment or to challenge existent knowledge. For example, in *Childhood in Crossroads* she makes use of psychological tests in ways that, as she wryly admits would "scarcely please psychologists" [5], drawing on them to illuminate both their efficacy and shortcomings and the possibilities they offered for a conversation between disciplines; as she puts it, "to lean on a century of insight and effort in one discipline to highlight interest in another." A quarrelsome stance, perhaps. Her research traces the influences on children's cognition of their environments and relationships, noting their ingenuity in conditions of apartheid's terrible constraints; the costs to the child of families sundered by the brutal political system; the ways that prevailing ideologies shape knowledge of the child, including through testing and the interpretation of results. She notes the delicacy of working with children—the ways that formal research processes may undo children's knowledge, rendering their worlds inaccurately. She suggests that working with

4

children demands a particular kind of attention, carefully focused through specifically devised methods.

On attention

Much of Pamela's work has been concerned with how to develop the modes of attention that enable the careful bringing-into-view of that which is taken-for-granted. In a recent article, she attributes her attention to evidence to her mentor and supervisor, Monica Wilson. She writes, "It is the vital importance of evidence that Monica taught me to keep in mind always. On what basis can one claim to know something?"[6] Reynolds' response—at least in my reading of it—has been to grant description great value, suggesting, "there can be no transformation without description."[7] Her argument here is that in the absence of a proper description of social realities—description of what is, rather than what people think ought to be—social interventions will flounder. Attention is a product of careful methodological formation and theoretical inventiveness.

I came to see Pamela's work as grappling with questions of attentiveness. My perspective was enlivened when Pamela recommended Al Alverez's work in literary studies. I had encountered Alvarez before in an entirely different context— my husband, a mountaineer and rock climber, was in thrall to *Feeding the Rat*, an account of Alvarez's love of mountaineering and the deep friendships that those who climb develop. In *The Writer's Voice*, however, Alvarez's writing is not of mountains but of literature. His work brought two different dimensions of my life into relation with one another. As a general rule, I read voraciously, with great enjoyment and very little recall. But a footnote in Alvarez's book—which Pamela had marked with her characteristic mark-up note; a circle for the beginning of a line of thought or a quote, a dash for its ending—remains with me.

> Etymologically, "attend" is a submerged metaphor. It comes from the Latin words *ad*, meaning "to" or "toward", and *tendere*, "to stretch". When I attend to you, I stretch my ears toward you.[8]

My mind returns frequently to this image. I have used it to think about what it might mean to pay attention when words are not being offered – when one is confronted by the silences of great suffering or of a refusal to admit pain lest it harm those with which it comes in touch, or renders one's world uninhabitable. Like so much of what I took from Pamela, Alvarez's footnote has come to be a placeholder for a way of thinking about the world and a method for how one might approach its mysteries and difficulties. And behind the retention of a footnote and its place in my thought there is a larger picture of relations that bring texts into conversation with lives. It was the Cape Town poet, Stephen Watson, a neighbour and friend, married to Tanya Wilson, the daughter of her dear friends Lindy and Francis, the latter, Monica Wilson's son, who had shared *The Writer's Voice* with Pamela. In her restless and generous way, Pamela had read and marked it up for what it might offer her thought and passed the work to me. I read her thought through her mark-ups and took from it what helped me to think through the puzzles of my work.

So we learn from those around us, or who came before, and take of what they offer what fits us for our tasks.

On method

I suggest that Reynolds' work offers a certain skepticism as a stance from which to isolate an object of inquiry; to subject it to a certain kind or mode of attention: a careful looking at from multiple directions—a mode of triangulation—in order to reach a truth. The questions that I see and experienced as being at stake in her work are "How might we see this matter? From what perspectives or from what institutions might we address the object in question in order to ascertain the truth or the veracity of its being or the veracity of its claims?" In *Dance Civet Cat*, her careful account of children's work in the Zambezi Valley, for example, Reynolds is clear that in order to understand children's work, we can't simply ask them about work, nor can we merely observe their work; we have to understand the broader context—which includes the extent to which adults fail to recognize what children do.[9] This is critical in order partly to combat our own lack of attention and partly to identify the way in which society requires a certain mode of forgetting or obscuring or failing to notice in order to continue to perpetuate its own foundational myths of adult labour and the making of the world.

The skeptical stance emerges most strongly in her work on South Africa's truth commission. Here was a commission established to ascertain "the truth" of what happened. I worked alongside Pamela as she excavated its process, viewing it—in her case—through the experiences of young activists who had fought against the state and in mine through ways that the Commission foregrounded a particular version of women's experiences (as or in relation to victims). It was tremendously demanding and sometimes dangerous work. In investigating youth activism, one had to confront sedimented and well-justified anger about white complicity with apartheid; to overcome distrust—or at least to be able to work alongside it; to engage deeply and fully with the discursive practices that the Commission put in place and the ways that these facilitated or disabled certain ways of knowing, and certain kinds of knowledge. Much of what I took from this tutelage concerned questions of how we name. In order to know the truth of what happened, she proposes, we have to be able to name it properly. In *War in Worcester*, rather than starting—as did the Commission—with the definition of "victim" given in human rights law and the Commission's foundational documents, Reynolds begins with the orientations and experiences of young people during apartheid. She asks the question the Commission failed to pose: "Was the relation between the apartheid state and activist children one in which children were viewed as combatants?" and answers it in the affirmative. In which case, this was not "unrest," as the state described it, but "war."

Arising from her methodological rigour is a set of questions concerning the most appropriate point of view to determine the truth of what happened. Thus the category of the child emerges as a mode, as a way of paying attention to experience, to the particular. In her earlier work on children and politics, Reynolds examines how the child grows to a political consciousness through ordinary socialization, which include interactions with the family and with the state. What she is very careful to document is how those take form and with what implications.

I suggest, then, that her method commences from a skeptical stance in order to ascertain or to move, through empirical attention and methodological rigour, toward an objective truth. For Reynolds, truth lies in how we name

8

things; the points at which we are able to ascertain fully what's at stake in description; and in the careful assessment of the adequacy of our terms for doing that description. A great deal of her preparatory work involves a very careful unpacking of concepts, of terminologies, of framings, of theoretical and philosophical orientations. "What is the version of the child that is at stake in any given description?" she asks. "How might we think about that more critically and more carefully, more accurately in relation to the empirical realities in which we find ourselves or in which our research participants find themselves?" "How might we arrive at a name that does justice to the experiences, or to the categories or to the modes of knowing that are at stake in the philosophical questions that we ask?" "What kinds of attention (the mode of inquiry we gloss as 'method') will generate the form of attentiveness best suited to answering the question of the place and being of the child in contemporary life forms?"

For Reynolds, coming to attention is demanding. It requires care in method. Dissatisfied with a singular perspective, distrusting of received wisdoms, she finds diverse ways to explore children's worlds, triangulating findings and all the while setting them in relation to the broader reaches of the social worlds in which children find themselves and make meaning of the world. In *Dance Civet Cat*, an account of children's work in the Zambezi Valley, for example, she develops careful methods for drawing out children's knowledge and practices, cross-referencing her observations with the recall of adults to show the extent to which children perform productive labour and simultaneously, the extent to which it goes unacknowledged as such by adults in children's ambits. Twenty-four hour recalls, spot observations, interviews, kinship tables, attendance at headmen's court proceedings; a wide range of methods is brought to bear on the project of recognizing children's work in contexts in which it is taken so for granted that it disappears from all kinds of accounting. Here, her method is rigorous, systemic, focused, objectivist. Yet, in *Traditional Healers and Childhood in Zimbabwe*, she proposes, "The topic calls for a creative methodology. Evidence must be caught on the wing."[10] And in *War in Worcester*, a simultaneous account of young people's courageous stance as anti-apartheid activists and the South African Truth and Reconciliation Commission's attempts to document the nature of apartheid's violence, Reynolds cites Lévinas as saying there is "no transparency possible in method." From this she deduces that "an approach to ethnographic fieldwork cannot be made completely explicit or justified as to why certain ways of proceeding were chosen."[11]

Between these positions—catching data on the fly, in the subtleties of interactions as healers attend to children in relation to others, including the dead; developing methods and approaches that in hindsight render clear the lineaments of social arrangements; or in the structured process of observations over time that characterized her earlier works— Reynolds develops a mode of ethnographic description that, as she describes it, "locates and describes children's situations using triangulation from different starting points." She continues, "Insights are drawn from different angles and contexts using a range of techniques to gain access to the inner worlds of children."[12] The result is always fine-grained analysis carefully set in relation to the broader socio-political context that shapes children's lives and practices. As she describes it in *Childhood in Crossroads*, she seeks insights into context so as "to weave the cloth upon which the pattern of the 7-year-olds' lives might stand in relief." [13] And in the beautiful *Lwaano Lwanyika, The Tonga Book of the Earth*, [14] a collaboration between Colleen Crawford Cousins and Reynolds, that wovenness of cultural form, social practice, material worlds and language's offerings is brought to life through the metaphor of the making of a home and the communities, knowledge, practices and histories that give it depth and meaning. A book of Tonga practice for Tonga people, it is also a delicate layering of image, metaphor and data that renders an empowering vision of what careful research might restore to people whose worlds have bore the brunt of political pressures.

Her assessment of children, childhoods and the contexts of their production is, by her own admission, quarrelsome. She takes issue with those who suggest, for example, that those who struggled against apartheid and bore the weight of the state's brutal response constitute a "lost generation." She is meticulous in her accounting of the child's experience, exposure, relationships and the possibilities that these afford. Her accounts are not romantic. Drawing from Foucault, she demands we discover "with what operation and criteria the child is introduced to the order of things" [15]; an accurate rendition of her own life's work and of the critical skills she seeks to impart to students. Her questions are thus not solely about children and the way they come to learn, but about how the world is ordered, how the child comes to know that ordering, what responsibilities adults and scholars have in the face of these orders, and, critically, about what children do when they learn that the world is unjust.

The latter is the core of her study of young political activists who came of age in the tumultuous period after the

Soweto youth uprisings of 1976. "Paring down the family"[16] asks what the family as an institution has borne and become in the midst of apartheid; what support and succor it might offer the young, especially those who stood against the wrath of the state. Her account of the violence of the state is chilling. Declaring that the apartheid state declared war on children, *War in Worcester* describes the content and consequences of that war for those who were at the heart of the storm. "With what tools does one come to political consciousness?" she asks. "How did children acquire their ethical orientations in a context of state aggression and social undoing?" "What have been the consequences to individuals and families of both state violence and the failure of the post-apartheid state properly to name and recognize the effects of violence on the young?" "What is the nature of betrayal and how might its ramifications be shored up, held in, perhaps even forgiven?" Her account is searing. Noting children's courage, both in acts of heroism and in the making of everyday social relations,[17] she is not sanguine about the forms of sociality that might arise—as she puts it, "There is almost an undoing of obligations toward certain children – a decomposition of nurturance."[18]

I currently supervise a young PhD student, Andile Mayekiso, who, mentored by Pamela, has completed a study of that decomposition and its effects on men.[19] His work draws on Pamela's prompts from a little known paper on male migrants in Cape hostels in the 1980s[20]; an account that describes migrants' despair at being separated from their children and their anxiety over what the family was made to become under apartheid's restrictions. Tracing the generational effects of a savage political-economy on the possibilities of family life, Mayekiso asks what becomes of fatherhood in contexts in which the means of social and economic independence are hard to grasp; where illness and poverty are the backdrop against which relationships are built; and where young men are unable to accomplish the ideals of masculinity that many hold dear. His research, conducted with young men who fathered children with HIV+ women, and building on an earlier project headed by Reynolds, has been demanding. He notes the erosion of sources of support; the ways that customary practices of initiation have been replaced by other, less socially productive modes of making valorized masculine forms; how men's desires to father are undercut by their inabilities to provide materially for their children. He describes how, in the absence of *intlawulo* ("damage payments" as they are commonly known—the traditional payment for impregnating a woman out of marriage) and marriage, women's families, and particularly grandmothers of the men's children, control and limit their access to the children they fathered. Against the grain of a literature that tends to discard men as wastrels, he shows how men desire to be respected as fathers, even as they note their failures in fathering. The account demonstrates the limitations in contemporary psychological models of attachment which prioritize the mother-child dyad and fail to acknowledge the role of wider social relationships in the making of childhood security, or to acknowledge the role men play in securing children into lineages and preserving their well-being through such incorporation.

Mayekiso draws on his own life experiences (such as discovering, shortly before his father's death, that the latter had children from relationships outside his formal "traditional" marriage; reflecting on his own experiences of initiation and social location) to situate and compare the lives

13

of men with whom he worked. Ostensibly "the same" in terms of "cultural practice," he shows how culture itself is made through everyday interactions that instantiate and valorize particular models of human well-being. This is one major difference between the works of current young scholars and those of an earlier generation; the researcher's self is not elided or included in the argument merely as a reflexive gesture that points to "positionality" and the power relations of knowledge-making (à la the *Writing Culture* debates of the late 1980s and the assumptions of "native anthropology" and "autoethnography"), but is actively engaged as a source of data, of nuancing an argument and developing its potential. It is difficult to do so, especially where one is describing relationships and worldviews that one takes for granted. A great deal of the work of supervision in this context was to historicize social explanations and moral accounts. For example, people with whom Andile conversed, including the men and their mothers themselves, frequently blame mothers for being too permissive, too absent, too "soft" on their sons. Rather than understanding how it was that historically women came to bear the burdens of being both mother and father in some contexts, and how these historical practices have become embedded in material contexts (access to and control over urban housing, for example) or social relations (such as solid or undermined links with paternal kinsmen), or cultural practices (whether or not men are initiated and how their status is perceived; how marriage and its consequences are understood), social explanations route through stereotypic gendered ideas. Andile himself held to these ideas until we were able carefully to unpick the histories of their production. "How have things come to be naturalized in this way?" "What contexts and

14

processes produce these practices as common-sense?" "How can we separate out different forms of assessment and evaluation (i.e. the intersections and necessary distances between our social knowledge and theoretical stance)?" These became animating questions of the write-up process. The result is an account that is textured by experience, intimate and comparative. It does not eschew judgment but is clear about the criteria for assessment. It does not presume similarity but draws on shared experience as a way to highlight social processes, including their differentiation in the everyday work of making masculinity.

On coming to language

I am conscious as I write this description of her work that I sound a little like Pamela. A student imbibes much from a mentor and guide, including their language, perhaps even characteristic tones, gestures, intonation. Academic learning, if it is not confrontational, is mimetic. Sometimes, perhaps of necessity, it is both. It matters from whence one's language comes and what one learns to do with it. St Augustine's account of how a child comes to language suggests it is in the pairing of a word and thing. Ludwig Wittgenstein takes issue with this, arguing that a child learns language *in use*. He offers the example of the apprentice learning to lay bricks—it is from the tone and gesture of the bricklayer and not simply his words, that the apprentice learns language as tool and technique. Reynolds cites Stanley Cavell's critique of Augustine's account which notes how isolated the child seems in the Augustinian account; for Cavell, the deficiency in this account is that the child seems unaccompanied by culture or social relations.[21] She offers a reading in which "the child comes to a political and ethical understanding, however immature and imperfect, through observing its culture and acting in accord with that understanding."[22] There is here space for the child's creativity in grappling with the world as it presents itself, in crafting it anew in changing conditions of possibility. She points out that there may be a gap between convention and what is[23], and that children navigate this space carefully and often in ways that are under-supported by the social institutions that ought ordinarily to protect them (the state, the family, etc.). The anthropological task is to account for both what is at hand and the ways that new futures are forged as children inhabit the world and make it their own.

If one imagines the mentorship relation as at least somewhat akin to the learning of a language and thus an orientation, as I've suggested above, tutelage then might be seen a mode of entering a relationship in which one consents to learn a new language and with it a way of being in the world; an orientation and an inheritance. But as her comment, "Do with it as you will" makes clear, that future is not *determined* by tools and predecessors.

If tutelage is an induction into language and its possibilities, including its pasts, what does it mean to inherit the scene of Anthropology's colonial entanglements and our predecessors' struggles with them? How are we to know what to turn toward or from? What of our inheritances are poisoned and what true? What is the relation of method to justice and to future possibility? Here, we might turn to Reynolds' work on children and traditional healing. Children, she says, "learn by observation, imitation and practice."[24] She suggests that "close tutorial relationships between healers and children are often formed and that it is the quality of learning that occurs within these relationships that gives the young entrée to the specialized sphere of divination and healing." And she notes that "many children learn … and are articulate about facets of their culture… Only some deepen that knowledge and immerse themselves in the learning processes that eventually lead to specialized practice…."[25]

That structured state of relationship that a university is pleased to call "supervision" is, or has the potential to be, so much more than its name implies. So, too, a research relationship. Responsibilities with unforeseen futures, they afford an openness that emerges, seeps sometimes, from the particularities of *these* relationships in *these* institutional forms: relationships that adhere to yet overflow the institutions designed to contain them. Supervised, one is extended into the world. Similarly, in ethnographic research, one is opened to the surprise and generosity that sustained attention across similarity and difference makes possible. New networks, different generations, a web of words that stretch over time. And with that, exclusions and dangers; boundaries drawn; lineaments of other relationships, older, that play out over time and thread through new relationships.

We are never fully free of the pasts of the generation that precedes us. One's knowing emerges initially in a voice not one's own entirely, ventriloquism or perhaps possession. How do we emerge as singular? Why do we come to imagine that our knowing is bereft of its pasts? What is the relation of our diverse voices and tasks to one another? Loyalty. Fidelity. To what does one owe allegiance? What is one willing to admit? To deny? To rebut? From whence comes this strength? They are questions that faced the young activists of whom we wrote in our respective works on South Africa's Truth Commission, and they are also questions that face a current generation of youth activists who seek to implement radical change in South Africa.

On coming to voice

What, as Alvarez would have it, is the voice that is truly our own? He suggests that to find it, one must first have mastered style; "a discipline you acquire by hard work."[26] Not rhetoric but "a voice with the whole weight of life, however young, behind it."[27] The philosopher Alfonso Lingis offers us this possibility: that when one enters communication, one speaks either in a depersonalized voice in which one's "visions and insights" are formulated "in terms of the common rational discourse"; that is, one speaks as "a representative"; or, he posits, "you find it is you, you saying something, that is essential."[28] As Alvarez notes, "The authentic voice may not be the one you want to hear."[29] One's own voice and its reception carries always the trace of a struggle, between the general and the specific, the personal and the historical.

Elsewhere, Lingis writes:

We dropped whatever we were engaged in and attend to someone who approached us. What we say picks up what she said. We pick up the tone, the vocabulary, the grammar, the rhetoric she uses, which answered to what others who have long passed by said and did. What we say awaits her confirmation or repudiation, or her question which our answer made possible.

We find ourselves contested in the midst of an endeavor; we answer for what we did and said. In answering now for what we said, we answer for what had been said to us and to which what we said was a response. We speak for those who

18

are no longer here to speak for themselves, who have passed by and who have passed away.

To respond is to commit ourselves to answer for what we answer. We address what we say to him or her who faces us, to what he or she will say and what he or she will be. We answer for when we will no longer be there.

Responsibility is not limited by what we have deliberately initiated and by the duration during which we pilot our enterprise with our own forces; responsibility is not authorship... To be responsible for our child is to have to answer now for that child's welfare when we will no longer be there.[30]

I take this as, in some measure, a description of the research encounter and also of the mode and effects of tutelage. From it, I draw four issues in relation to the task at hand: We are shaped by what we learn of one another through attention and communication; our response to one another is drawn forth as imperative; we are responsible for the now and the past that led to it and the future that will arise from it; responsibility has well-being as its end and extends beyond our capacities. Lingis suggests that responsibility is tied to the imperative to answer for the child when we are no longer there. This dictum, Levinasian in scope, ties us bodily to the things of the world; into a future we birth but will not see. It takes courage to pursue. Part of that courage must surely be naming and renaming; seeing the world from a position and offering the right name of things so that new possibilities emerge.

On protest and possibility

Young South Africans have long known this. As Reynolds has documented, many young people, supported by elders, have struggled against systems of power to identify new possibilities in the world. I have written this article slowly, between 2015 and 2016, in the midst of student protests that have seen the closure or disruption of more than half of South Africa's 23 public universities; reactive and violent responses by police in ways reminiscent of apartheid's brutal suppression; and massive solidarity among students and some staff at universities across the country. These have consolidated into a demand for free higher education in the context of diminishing state investment in real terms in that sector. Although state expenditure on education is among the highest in the world (approximately six percent of the national budget), state investment in Higher Education constitutes only approximately 0.7% of the budget. The rate of support for higher education is considerably lower than in other countries on the continent, many far poorer than South Africa. Across the country, students have been protesting what they see as on-going exclusions of poor, young black youth from the centres of education and from debt-free futures. Their protests are not unlike "service delivery" protests and state responses that have rocked the country[31] but with one significant difference; they have mobilized nationally rather than locally, across differences of class, race and gender, and confronted the state in its places of power— the Parliamentary Buildings in Cape Town and the Union Buildings in Pretoria. And they have spread: similar protests have occurred across universities in the UK and USA among others. In so doing, they have framed a youth uprising that is as much about the future as the present. They criticize their forebears for having "bought into" the "myth" of the rainbow nation instantiated in the "transition period" of the mid 1990s, the period in which Pamela and I studied so carefully its signature institution, the Truth and Reconciliation Commission[32] and its failings to recognize the roles of youth and women in the struggle against injustice and violence. Recognizing the weight of debt they will carry for their education notwithstanding state assistance in the form of loans and grants through NSFAS, the students of #RhodesMustFall and #FeesMustFall have offered a powerful critique of the ways that the neoliberal economic policies enacted in the post-apartheid period nevertheless perpetuate racialized capital and privilege, forcing the poor to carry the burden of debt.

The protests have drawn huge numbers of students. Some twelve thousand young people marched on the Union Buildings in Pretoria on 23 October 2015. They were violently dispersed by Public Order Police. Universities were "disrupted"; some closed. Some university authorities called in police and private security guards. Exams in some institutions were halted. The student movements, like those of earlier decades in South Africa, have generated intense discussion about the nature of the post-apartheid order; the ways that it fails adequately to support young people into the future; the limits of transitional justice; the rights—and wrongs—of state power and the ways it is brought to bear on enabling or limiting young people's futures.

In *War in Worcester*, Reynolds cites Foucault's concern with understanding governmentalisation: particularly his exploration of "how not to be governed like that…" Reynolds states, presciently, "The question for today and tomorrow is the governance of children, how it fits into current notions and responsibilities of the state, and how it is theorized and acted upon by citizens." [33] "Service delivery protests," state violence, the failure of the education system, the formation of new political parties, the ongoing undoing of family life by economic erosions, the massacre of mineworkers at Marikana, and now the student protests raise this question viscerally. Social anger points to an unresolved question about how to craft the future, and what futures are at stake. What has become clear from the radical critique some students have offered, often from a Black Consciousness and intersectoral vantage, is that extant modes of analysis and representation are insufficient, even harmful. Eschewing as violent the texts that depict Africans as Other, abject or in terms of intractable loss, they demand capaciousness in scholarship; work that is life giving.

In conclusion

Anthropology, and its signature method, ethnography, has—rightly—had its share of critique in postcolonial Africa and in post-apartheid South Africa. The role the discipline played in the formation of the apartheid state's imaginary was profound and tragic. Reynolds has dedicated her intellectual world to a record of both the destruction wrought and the possibilities that remain. As we struggle with questions of how to grapple with disciplinary legacies, including its writings, it behooves us to ask what possibilities lie in what is known, albeit partially, in limited or limiting ways. As Reynolds herself notes, "Questions can be raised as to how South Africans recognize a canon in anthropology, how they claim a founding knowledge and hence can value a continuing tradition in the discipline." [34] This requires a mode of reading,

22

of critical alertness. We cannot be complacent in relation to what we receive.

I have come to imagine anthropology a mode of orienting; specificities that are built from the matter of life as it surrounds and embeds us, rather than solely as a matter of content and canon. The disciplines that have long interested Pamela—anthropology, philosophy, psychology—are powerful. She has demonstrated—often through using one against the other— the ways that attentiveness, care in naming, accounting and a reading against the grain can reveal the lives of children in particular, and about the order of things in general.

*****

In thinking about the effects of a relationship that has shaped me profoundly as scholar and person, about the index card's injunction, the affordances of scholarly work and the intimacies of friendship, about the question of what it might take to live, aware of and grateful for what has been offered and responsible for what has been received, I have found Alfonso Lingis's ideas useful. He writes:

> In taking our place at a post others have vacated, we see in the arrangement left on things not only the diagram of their skills that can be reinscribed on our forces but also the outline of singular enterprises that they did not have the power to realize: possibilities they left behind, for others, for us…. [W]e find what our lives are for and find our own courage.[35]

Perhaps one might say that the greatest gift a mentor— supervisor, colleague, friend—can offer is the example of her own courage, suggesting but not defining the route to one's own. I wonder how history will judge us.

Notes

[1] Pamela Reynolds, *War in Worcester* (New York: Fordham University Press, 2013).

[2] In an interview published in *Altérités* in 2010, Veena Das describes the work of time as enabling one to be attentive to difficulty without being paralyzed. She states, "if one puts forward one's view in the world, even if it's fallible, then other voices will join, either to correct or to amplify, or to revise one's view." I take this as an ethical injunction to scholars and at the same time, a corrective to those who would assume the singular can be isolated from the collective and from the times in which knowledge and relationship are produced. Pamela Reynolds was Veena Das's M. Litt. student. Pamela introduced me to Veena's work in the mid-1990s. Their scholarship has been profoundly influential in my work. F. Turcot diFruscia, "Listening to Voices: An interview with Veena Das." *Altérités*, 7(1): 136-145.

[3] Pamela Reynolds, *Childhood in Crossroads* (Cape Town: David Philip, 1989), 5.

[4] Reynolds, *Childhood in Crossroads*, 9.

[5] Reynolds, *Childhood in Crossroads*, 4.

[6] Pamela Reynolds, "Gleanings and leavings: Encounters in hindsight", in *Inside African Anthropology: Monica Wilson and Her Interpreters*, A. Bank and L. Bank, eds. (Cambridge: Cambridge University Press, 2013), 308-320, 318.

[7] Pamela Reynolds, "The ground of all making: state violence, the family and political activists," in *Violence and Subjectivity*, V. Das, A.

Kleinman, M. Ramphele and P. Reynolds, eds. (Berkeley: University of California Press, 2000), 141-170, 145.

[8] Al Alvarez, *The Writer's Voice* (London: Bloomsbury: London, 2004), 16.

[9] Pamela Reynolds, *Dance Civet Cat* (London: Zed Books, 1991).

[10] Pamela Reynolds, *Traditional healers and childhood in Zimbabwe* (Athens, OH: Ohio University Press, 1996), xxxiv.

[11] Reynolds, *War in Worcester*, 3.

[12] Reynolds, *Childhood in Crossroads*, xxxix.

[13] Reynolds, *Childhood in Crossroads*, 10.

[14] Pamela Reynolds and Colleen Crawford Cousins, *Lwaano Lwanyika, The Tonga Book of the Earth* (London: Panos, 1994).

[15] Reynolds, *Childhood in Crossroads*, 198.

[16] Pamela Reynolds, *Paring Down the Family: The Child's Point of View* (Pretoria: HSRC, 1995), 145.

[17] Reynolds, *Traditional healers and childhood in Zimbabwe*.

[18] Reynolds, *Traditional healers and childhood in Zimbabwe*, 143.

[19] Andile Mayekiso, *"Ukuba yindoda kwelixesha" ("To be a man in these times"): Fatherhood, marginality and forms of life among young men in Gugulethu, Cape Town.* PhD dissertation under examination, University of Cape Town, unpublished).

[20] Reynolds, "Men without children," Carnegie Conference Paper 5 (Cape Town, 1984), 12-28.

[21] Reynolds, *War in Worcester*, 15.

[22] *ibid.*

[23] Reynolds, *Traditional healers and childhood in Zimbabwe*, 142.

[24] Reynolds, *Traditional healers and childhood in Zimbabwe*, xxxviii.

[25] *ibid.*

[26] Alvarez, *The Writer's Voice*, 20.

[27] Alvarez, *The Writer's Voice*, 9.

[28] Alphonso Lingis, *The Community of Those Who Have Nothing in Common* (Bloomington, IN: Indiana University Press, 1994), 116.

[29] Alvarez, *The Writer's Voice*, 29.

[30] Alphonso Lingis, *The Imperative* (Indiana University Press: Bloomington, 1998), 13.

[31] On May 15, 2015, Police Minister Nathi Nhlekho told Parliament that police resources had been committed to 14,740 service delivery protests. *The Citizen* May 15, 2015.

[32] Reynolds, *War in Worcester*; Fiona C. Ross, *Bearing Witness: Women and the Truth and Reconciliation Commission in South Africa* (London: Pluto Press, 2003).

[33] Reynolds, *War in Worcester*, 15.

[34] Reynolds, *War in Worcester*, 315.

[35] Lingis, *The Imperative*, 141.

Cuts of Various Depths
A few scenes of learning from Pamela Reynolds

Todd Meyers

> I was aware that the teaching of drawing was being
> stopped almost 30 years ago. And I always said, "The
> teaching of drawing is the teaching of looking." A lot of
> people don't look very hard.
>
> David Hockney[1]

There are two pieces of art in Pamela Reynolds' home that
hold meaning for me. The first is a lithograph by the British
painter David Hockney entitled *Black Tulips* (1980).
Hockney's paintings and drawings, especially his pool
paintings from the late 1960s, are typically playful, sexual and
comical, ever-changing in style without question of
authorship, exact but not obsessive. The pool paintings are
filled with colours washed flat by the light of an intense
California sun pressed against mid-century homes inhabited
by literati and hustlers. Pamela has a lithograph from this
period of Hockney's career, but I never gave it much thought.
Its blue lines are too symmetrical, too cold. It is a work that is
out of place anywhere other than with itself.

Black Tulips is, by contrast, inviting, maybe even a little
seductive. A simple planter sits atop a small table, patterned
skirt and flowers lifting in the breeze from an open window
or door somewhere out of the scene. The objects suggest the

movement of a figure. The buff-coloured paper is warm and essential to the work. The tulips are drawn with long, confident strokes made in black ink, possibly with a sumi brush. *Those lines.* Those lines executed with such confidence––lines not striving for anything. I would try to sit myself across from *Black Tulips*, to face it from the other side of Pamela's broad pear wood dining table (itself a work of art, rippled with yellow and amber and tan grains), when she and her students would gather every few weeks to discuss works-in-progress over rare steaks and red wine. I cannot be sure anyone noticed or cared. I would lean on *Black Tulips* to steady myself, to avoid tripping over words, to escape the inevitable rush of thought unleashed in an unfailingly clumsy combination of unknowing and brashness performed by the graduate student. I hoped (less consciously than I make it seem now) that those lines would tether me, weigh me down by adding ballast of decided, discreet movements, never exhibiting more than is necessary, not for protection but for purpose. After all, isn't this how I have come to regard Pamela Reynolds' words and teachings—decided, purposeful? *Black Tulips* is a model, an object lesson still present in my mind's eye, hanging in the dining room of Pamela's Baltimore row house. There's a kind of flawlessness to it—seen but just beyond grasp.

The second is an etching and aquatint by Pablo Picasso entitled *Peintre et Modele au Tabouret* (1963). Picasso: genius, misogynist, occasionally hackneyed, self-obsessed, an artist whose character is so far out of alignment with Pamela's as to represent its opposite. But *Peintre et Modele* is more useful than *Black Tulips*. What it lacks in elegance is made up by instruction. *Black Tulips* is a conclusion, the result of practice, the product of rehearsal after rehearsal; *Peintre et Modele* is the labour of that practice. It is work exhausted from workings and reworkings. There are lines made with resolve. There are others that appear completely arbitrary, executed against form.

Peintre et Modele is not grand, but for being so slight it is wildly inconsistent as the viewer's eye travels between the model and artist, separated by the tilted meridian of an easel. Lines compose the model in the left hemisphere, fluid and bright, perhaps created in a single motion with no hatch marks to find her naked form. And on the right, the artist is a constellation of blotches and haphazard lines, cuts of various depths never quite arriving at a shape—dark and obscured. Gilles Deleuze writes about the paintings of Francis Bacon as Figures made intense and distorted as an attempt to grasp sensation-as-form in the containers of space Bacon built within the frames of his paintings.[2] But Picasso's "painter" is not a Figure in a movement of becoming, in the creative struggle for and with the sensation of being: he is the product of a different frustration. Each mark is a fresh impediment to work around. There is no attempt at new stylistic forms, no experiment with content. So why persist?

Peintre et Modele was tucked in a low opening under the bookshelves in Pamela's fourth floor study, framed by rows of fiction, poetry, theory, and anthropology. A swirl of privilege and foreboding and promise was felt when discussing work with Pamela in her study, and I never forgot each time ascending the stairs that most climbers perish on the decent. We would talk about work, and at some point (not every time, but often) we would talk about *Peintre et Modele*. There was rarely duplication between previous discussions because, at least for my part, my thoughts never fully arrived at any conclusion about the piece. I, too, was still

29

working it out, a mix of invention and improvisation. None of this was rehearsed and it was such a pleasure. To be clear, these conversations were far from vague. We talked about the anthropologist and the artist, carving away, working and reworking, exposing, concealing, creating… How many times did Picasso return to *Peintre et Modele* to confront its inexactitude? If the work has value beyond the fame of its creator, it is found in its ability to make bare the action of the artist without resting on the resolve of that action. *Peintre et Modele* is a portrait of the painter as anthropologist: obsessive, undecided, mess-making, prone to destroy one form to yield another, and returning, always returning.

*****

There are others in this volume who will detail pedagogical moments that inspire, challenge, and inform— and while I would like to add to the chorus, I instead ask for indulgence about a different kind of moment. It comes as the expression of intellectual generosity in thinking alongside a student, on terms offered by that student and his work, in order to draw out hidden threads that even a decade later the student can only begin to appreciate.

Pamela penned a postscript to an essay I wrote when I was her pupil, which she entitled "Yes (but not yet)."[3] My essay was about work I had conducted with a family in a neighbourhood in Southwest Baltimore, not far from where Pamela lived. The focus was on a woman, Beverly, who was in the throes of caring for her family, caring and not caring for herself, struggling with multiple illnesses, addiction, chronic pain, economic insecurity, etc.—and who, at some point in the course of my time knowing her, decided she was

30

dying. No one had told her she was dying. Beverly determined that, with all that had happened to her, all that surrounded her, she had made a turn in her life toward dying. I sought to trace that turn. Here are Pamela's words, reflecting on and amplifying what I had written—words which, for reasons of space and editorial privilege, never appeared in print alongside my essay.

In Joan Didion's[4] account of the year of magical thinking through which she lived after the death of her husband, she uses as a refrain the first words she wrote after he had died,

> *Life changes fast.*
> *Life changes in the instant.*
> *You sit down to dinner and life as you know it ends.*
> *The question of self-pity.*

She considered adding three words,

> *Life changes in the instant*
> *The ordinary instant.*

But she did not: "I saw immediately that there would be no need to add the word 'ordinary', because there would be no forgetting it: the word never left my mind." Later, Didion recalled the words spoken by Episcopalians at the graveside, "*In the midst of life we are in death.*" She experienced her husband's death as having been an abrupt intrusion on the everyday (he collapsed as they sat down to eat supper together and died from a massive heart attack) but, in retrospect, she realizes that his experience was one of dying in living. In contrast, Beverly's experience is not of dying in living but of living in dying. She seems to mourn her own death before it occurs: to grieve for the loss of living while living.

Stanley Cavell suggests that Emerson makes his demand for "a recounting of what has hitherto been taken to count" to ensure that historians do not uncritically accept "the received significance" of events as they document the past. [5] In this paper, Todd Meyers poses the question: what is taken to count in an analysis of the care given by medical institutions to poor, chronically ill patients? He listens as Beverly tells him what counts in her reassessment of her life as she handles chronic illness while filling her role as the pivotal member of a four-generation kin group.

Meyers carefully documents Beverly's understanding that "she has been dying more than she has been living" to suggest that increasingly for some people "illness and dying are no longer processes" but that disease, "like death, is marked by an arrival; it is one of many destinations along the landscape of human health". He initiates a recounting of what has hitherto been taken to count in the alignment of meaning and experience within the medical imagination. The paper's epigraph is, "Death has not required us to keep a day free" and nor, one could add having read the paper, does it promise to leave a day free of its prophesy (promise?) once chronic illness takes hold of somebody whose life is already a struggle.

I shall, in this brief note, point to some of the uses to which ethnography has been put in the exploration of a patient's requirements of, responses to and maneuvers within a fragmented medical institution. Ethnographic methods are used to bring to the fore the complexity of institutional transactions that people living in poverty are obliged to entertain. In recording one woman's reflections on particular events relating to her illness, search for care and family responsibilities, Meyers demonstrates how the management of illness results in changes having to be made in social arrangements and how the process instigates reconsiderations of self. In the process of learning about this, the ethnographer interrogates the expectations and assumptions that inform the ideas that, in part, shape medical scientific practices.

The author has chosen to structure the presentation of the material and the argument to reflect the way in which Beverly sketched her thoughts, scrabbling time, bringing him to see the architecture of her understanding. She seemed to anticipate in him an audience and, in the presence of Meyers's interest and reticence, assembled an account of the pain entailed in being ill, in negotiating medical, legal and welfare institutions, and in bearing responsibilities. As Emmanuel Lévinas says, pain "requires a dialogical nature"[6].

The paper is about connections (between illness, dying, living and clinical treatment) and dimensions (social, individual, institutional) that Beverly makes in contemplating her predicament. In her description of time, one occurrence does not lead inexorably to another but can be slipped in like a page in a loose-leaf diary altering the perspective she has on life and care. The paper raises questions about how a chronically ill patient sees her various illnesses and her progression towards death and, therefore, what choices she sees herself as having in handling them in relation to her other obligations (whether to spend money on medications; or on securing her rights to care for her grandchildren; or on co-payments for a visit to a clinic that is likely to lead to hospitalization; or in selecting among symptoms the most pressing that may benefit from a visit to a clinic; and which clinics to avoid because she has overstepped her benefits); and how her sense of self enters the equation. Beverly's engagement in spheres of the domestic and the medical provide insights into the nexus of health, poverty, family and medication. The ethnographic framework of the paper enables us to focus on the repetitions and discontinuities that illness injects into a single life in terms that draw attention to concerns beyond the measure of illness.

Ethnographic methods are used to describe the manner in which experiences are layered one upon another and, in the process of assigning them meaning, are shuffled not necessarily in accord with the strict passage of time. Meyers captures Beverly's continuing reconsideration of her life as she interleaves the experiences of the everyday – the nuances of relationships, the contingencies of events in the family, and the labour of existence – into episodes of chronic illness.

Marshall Sahlins[7] curtly reminds us that, "ethnography is Anthropology, or it is nothing". Meyers's ethnographic description offers the phenomenological experience of one person as she negotiates life and the fractured medical health care system in a poor area. It was as an ethnographer (even when piqued at being duped into usefulness) that Meyers came to recognize "the simultaneous newness and repetition of crisis and recovery" that characterized Beverly's experiences. In depicting ethnographic encounters, he draws the reader's attention to the relationship between illness and dying through Beverly's efforts to balance critical episodes of illness *and* the daily management of its nagging presence within the ordinary pursuits of survival. He invites the reader to acknowledge how Beverly continually reflects on the alteration of her consciousness of self as it is wrought in the telling of dying in the present.

Perhaps sharing this postscript will appear self-serving, and this wouldn't be too far from the truth. Just as I attempted to "see the architecture of [Beverly's] understanding," Pamela cared enough to inspect that scaffolding which held my thoughts. I am currently preoccupied with this writing again, after returning to Baltimore to reconnect with Beverly and her family, and after finding that she had died and that my return also required an unexpected form of repair. I am still making hatch marks around this woman, attempting to find ethnographic form without betraying that form. Early on I shared with Pamela that I wanted to turn around each time I drove from my house to visit Beverly (at her home, at a hospital, in an emergency room). I anticipated the chaos and discomfort—the awkwardness—of entering whatever situation awaited. Somehow I had hoped she would confirm what I felt, namely that this was all wrong, that I was wrong, and that I should stop, in effect letting me off the hook. Her response was the opposite, an acknowledgment. Indeed, this was the feltness of a "nagging presence within the ordinary pursuits of survival."

There is something to be said for marks that endeavor to find a form rather than to make a clear outline. I never introduced Pamela to Beverly. And still, she engaged in a labour of thought in which I still toil. Pamela models thought. Now I try to participate in the similar labour with students, not to teach (what lessons do I have to share?), but to think aloud, to think alongside, to scratch at the grain of thought and image in their work, and to reflect back the imprudent and wonderful labour of anthropology.

Pamela shared lessons as we prepared dinner and cleaned up afterwards. One learns to think aloud and in the midst of other tasks. There is no *imperceptible influence*; I feel every mark. But there are indirect lessons: the pompous are made foolish. A room can be made silent with a turn of phrase, or unexpected pathways of conversation are opened. In her scholarship and mentorship, the powerless are reminded of their capacitates for creativity, observation, speech, and most of all, the significance of their labour, their strokes and lines. One learns to trust words and respect their power of truth and diverting truth, as anthropology becomes a lens through which we begin to see our works and our worlds, even or especially in return.

Notes

[1] Interview, "David Hockney on canvassing for new ideas," *National Post*, December 15, 2011.

[2] Gilles Deleuze, *Francis Bacon: The Logic of Sensation*, trans. Daniel W. Smith. (Minneapolis: University of Minnesota Press, 2005).

[3] Todd Meyers, "A Turn Towards Dying: Presence, Signature, and the Social Course of Chronic Illness in Urban America," *Medical Anthropology* 26 (2007): 205-227.

[4] Joan Didion, *The Year of Magical Thinking* (New York: Knopf, 2005).

[5] Stanley Cavell, *Cities of Words: Pedagogical Letters on the Register of the Moral Life* (Cambridge: Harvard University Press, 2005), 256.

[6] Emmanuel Lévinas, "Useless Suffering," trans. Michael B. Smith and Barbara Harshav, in *Entre nous: Thinking-of-the-Other* (New York: Columbia University Press, 1998), 91–101.

[7] Marshall Sahlins, *Waiting for Foucault, Still* (London: Prickly Paradigm Press, 2002), 12.

3

Anthropology and the Development of Conscience
Reflections on the work of Pamela Reynolds

Thomas Cousins

> Persons who cannot use words, or gestures, in these ways with you may yet be in your world, but perhaps not of your flesh.
>
> Stanley Cavell, *The Claim of Reason*[1]

Here I revisit four books by Pamela Reynolds in order to reflect on what it means to grow up with(in) anthropology and to respond to the difficulty of inheritance and bequest. The line tracked through the four works is concerned with what it means to inherit a particular sensibility, call it politics, or ethics, and the implications this has for becoming a student of the projects of others, which is one way to name anthropology. The idea I am responding to here concerns the ways in which we come into relation with others, freighted in South Africa by the particulars of a social logic that has suggested that certain others do not share in our substance, or are not part of our flesh. The four works offer a picture of how it is that we, at least in the southern African history of violence, come into a mutuality of being[2] whose necessary or life-giving wounding capacity is occluded by the particular violence of apartheid and its entailments. I take the opportunity to consider a picture of learning and inheritance that stitches anthropology to the worlds of those who inhabit its disciplinary dreams. I want to suggest that Pamela's work provides a pedagogy for an anthropology of the development of conscience. The counterpoint that informs my sense of coming into relation(s) with the books and the subjects who inhabit them is my own childhood and initiation into anthropology.

I start from a suggestion by Stanley Cavell on how language depends on our ability to project words into new contexts. He describes the resulting difficulty of securing the meaning of one's words and thus the sense of achieving mutual understanding through language. I wonder to what extent such a notion works for the uptake of anthropology? In suggesting such a comparison, I make myself vulnerable to the accusation of a banal or inaccurate comparison. While Michael Lambek and others speak of "ordinary ethics" from a similar conceptual orientation, I take the challenge of identifying a "shared form of life" or "mutual attunement" as a particular difficulty when considering "teaching", not in the abstract, but in terms of my own struggle with anthropology. Is anthropology like language in that we should speak not of acquiring it but in terms of a "bequest"? Cavell says, "we are stingy in what we attempt to inherit."[3] Or is it like poetry, as "the second inheritance of language"?[4]

> If learning a first language is thought of as the child's acquiring of it, then poetry can be thought of as the adult's acquiring of it, as coming into possession of his or her own language, full citizenship. (Thoreau distinguishes along these lines between what he calls the mother tongue and the father tongue.) Poetry thereby celebrates its language by making it a return on its birth, by reciprocating.[5]

38

I suspect that the reciprocation that motivates this essay is more prosaic than poetic.

The four projects, which include books and related articles, are *Childhood in Crossroads: Cognition and Society in South Africa* (1989); *Traditional Healers and Childhood in Zimbabwe* (1996); *Dance Civet Cat* (1991); and *War in Worcester* (2013). Their years of publication do not align with the chronology of fieldwork, but this is the case for much of the field. In following these four works, I am interested in tracing the development of a notion of conscience in order to reflect on my own role as a teacher, now, and the ways in which I might be implicated in the development of conscience in another generation of anthropology students. My implication is also my complicity on both sides of the equation: an endorsement of anthropology's methods and values, which on the one hand has been made to answer for its responsibility in establishing the order of things – for the conditions of possibility – for colonial domination and apartheid regimes of difference in southern Africa; and on the other, has demonstrated the techniques of equivocation by which to destroy those regimes of oppression. Simultaneously, this setting provides the grounds for a coming into relation, for establishing kinship in the strong sense of the word, among people rent apart by exploitation, racial theories of difference, and torture.

Insofar as Pamela's works provide not only an anthropology of the development of conscience but also a pedagogy, they do so by focusing on the experience of the young under conditions of severe duress, of momentous political change, and of intense social judgement. The pedagogy I wish to reflect on here is not only found in the content of the books, but also emerges in the manner in which it is conducted and composed. Without making recourse to an argument about "ethnography in the way of theory" [6], as João Biehl does, the demonstration of how to pay attention to the young and to the development of conscience is embodied in its very execution.

My aim is to trace a line through four ethnographic projects in order to draw out what I consider to be critically at stake in the particular orientations that Pamela has developed, not only for anthropology in general but in relation to the young and the social and political contexts that frame my own teaching today. The relations between these works and the life-making projects of the young they describe; my own training and initiation into a certain kind of anthropology; and the students at the university where I currently teach form an armature of points of articulation. They are the joints that establish a scaffolding for a picture of learning and creative response to conditions not of one's own choosing. They necessarily place at stake my own blind spots, prejudices and tendencies, as well as those of the subjects who risk themselves in making themselves available to the anthropological reach, and those of the students of such projects. Equally, the texts, worlds, and readers of anthropological monographs are jointed and articulated by a grammar of learning that mirrors the question of how one learns (of) conscience. The concern with conscience that Pamela develops over the course of these works provides a way to think this armature, less as an abstract or "merely" philosophical concern than as a worldly, grounded matter of how ethical life is continued and reproduced in the midst of, and after, revolution. Zezuru healers have a concept of "*hana*" – heartbeat, conscience – or purity of heart that frames their selection by the spirits.[7] In *War in Worcester*, the authors discuss the concept of *"imfobe"*, variously translated as morality, virtue, goodness, and grace. As one of Pamela's collaborators Xolile Dyabooi puts it, "goodness of heart to the extreme".[8] Pamela examines,

> The critical self-consciousness to which [the young men] subjected their experiences and decisions... I contend that they had to acquire self-knowledge and to act, however imperfectly, in accord with a code of ethics, however shakily manufactured, in order to survive and to direct local operations, however impromptu and small in scale and effect. I am attempting to draw out some facets of the reach for self-knowledge and the formulation of ethics, or at least to suggest an aspect of what we might need to know if we are to understand the experiences of children and youth who become embroiled in conflict. I do not mean to suggest that young leaders were innocent.[9]

Each project is informed by a distinct set of thinkers; the particular way in which their ideas and the ethnography are braided gives Pamela's writing a distinct texture. In *Childhood in Crossroads*, it is a playful use of Piaget's notions of childhood development that provides the foil for a description of apartheid's effect on childhood. In *Traditional Healers and Childhood in Zimbabwe*, it is Freud and Jung, Gaston Bachelard and Henry James. In *Dance Civet Cat*, Quentin Meillassoux, Claude Levi-Strauss, Umberto Eco, and Elizabeth Colson. And in *War in Worcester*, Emmanuel Lévinas provides a framework for considering one's responsibility to others, and understanding how the men can be seen to have "paid attention to moral behaviour and the work involved in it."[10]

It strikes me that to write in this mode, about the young under apartheid, requires some degree of irony if one is to entertain the gory details of the violence and betrayals that constitute these revolutionary periods; irony in the ambivalent philosophical sense of living on after knowledge of betrayal or violation. In *War in Worcester*, Nana Khohlokoane, one of the men with whom Pamela worked, talks about such irony in an interview with Fiona Ross cited in the book:

> Regrettably, we wish we had taken heed of the words of Nkwame Nkrumah [the first president of postcolonial Ghana] that the struggle should not be a means to exploit women. We sort of wanted emotional comfort, while we did not trust them. That's the, you know, irony of the situation. We wanted them to comfort us, to sleep, have sex, and feel relieved of the pressure, and at the same time we did not speak to them about what is troubling us, the emotional traumas that were burning inside us. Women were seen as potential informers.[11]

Life without conscience is unimaginable; and yet the givenness of conscience in anthropology, as much as in social life, must surely remain a question to be explored in the concrete rather than as an assertion or *a priori*. While many anthropologists talk of a sensibility or orientation to ethnography that cannot be specified by so many rules or instructions, others want to assert that the values, styles, and feeling for the game can be made sensible, if not rational, and thereby better transmitted. Pamela's work with and on the young suggests the truth of both possibilities: that ethnography can be learned, and that the stakes of such disciplined endeavours emerge not from logical or rational rules but from particular crises that confront the living and

42

knowledge of life.[12] Conscience, perhaps as a particular capacity or power, is not one thing, but touches on many aspects of life, and it is critically in question in Pamela's ethnographic work on the young during and after revolutionary violence in southern Africa. In relation to recent calls for a more robustly political de-colonial anthropology, what place is there for the thickly described efforts of the young, specifically young Black South Africans and Zimbabweans, and what effects does such an archive have on those calls?

I grew up in the shadow of the children that speak from the pages of Pamela's ethnographies. It is their shadows that haunt our postcolonial forgetting in the decades after war.

Childhood in Crossroads

Childhood in Crossroads: Cognition and Society in South Africa is based on Pamela's doctoral fieldwork conducted between 1979-1981. The study was an experiment that asked how children come to know in a context of insecurity. She studied fourteen seven-year-old children in Crossroads, a "squatter settlement" on the edge of Cape Town, infamous for its history of forced removals and violence meted out by the apartheid government. It was a provocative and inspired project: to take aim at psychology's assumptions about child cognitive development and apartheid society's notions of black children's cognitive capacities and, simultaneously, to reveal the effects of apartheid's violent policies on the most vulnerable members of South African society. The study encompassed a wide range of concerns: time, space, kinship, dreams, and order(ing). At a time when there was a scarcity of publications in South African anthropology on the young, the book is a detailed examination of children's creative, emotional, and relational responses to the destruction of ordinary life under apartheid.[13]

I excerpt two examples on materials, play and space that are reflected in the research I carried out years later:

> The children had very few personal possessions. Among them they owned one broken bicycle, two broken wind-up cars, one ball, one length of skipping twine and some hoopla wire.... It is impossible to say what impact the lack of possessions had on their learning. No doubt the lack of opportunity to manipulate, order and construct things that were made out of materials uniform in shape, colour or texture towards particular ends rendered the children less confident when faced with formal tasks in a test situation. Similarly, their lack of exposure to pictures and written stories made the introduction of reading and writing a more complicated process. However, their use of rhythm, their repertoire of songs, their own song compositions and their ingenuity in play warn against placing too great an emphasis on their lack of possessions. The children's own activities and the objects and plants available in the environment offered a rich base upon which educational skills such as classification and numeracy could have been founded.[14]

Although there are many other angles opened by the project, here the material invites a critique of the conditioning of self and the imposition of a horizon of possibility by the evil of apartheid, rendered in terms of a child's reach:

> Ambitions: Four girls want to be nurses and one a teacher. None of them saw any obstacle in reality to prevent them from achieving their goals. Another girl wanted to be a Western-

trained doctor or a driver, but she granted that in reality she would probably be a char or a baker. A seventh girl wanted to be a factory worker and the last girl a clerk who could type ... ; both supposed that they would really be chars. Of the boys, two wanted to work in a factory, two wanted to be clerks, and two said that they would be drivers.[15]

In 1984, I wrote a letter to my grandmother stating that I wanted to be farmer, like my father, or an astronaut. At that point, my father worked for agricultural extension services for the Zimbabwean government, before beginning postgraduate studies on communal area grazing schemes. He later became a professor of land and agrarian studies. Many years later I found myself training in anthropology, and studying nutrition and labour.

In her book on looking at the play and songs of children in Crossroads, Reynolds offers a subtle critique of the criteria used to measure cognitive development, and hence, the racialized logic meant to justify the limiting measures:

> Few matters that relate to the development of cognition can be studied in isolation. A child's use of space, particularly in play, reflects the child's liberty and wealth, which reflects the nature of the economic and political realities of that child's society. An obvious point but one grossly neglected by those who write about cognitive development. I do not mean to imply that privileged children in the South African context use play or develop notions of space the are necessarily superior but only that the criteria against which they are measured should not be biased.[16]

She notes the popular forms of play amongst the children making houses and roads in the sand and cars out of wire elaborate the observations on possessions:

> The houses varied in the complexity of their design, the variety of materials used and in the number of the children involved. For example, one girl playing alone etched the plan of a house in the sand using two plastic spoons; in contrast, thirteen children built a village in the dunes using a wide selection of scraps, leaves and household items. In the latter example, two girls began to build on a high soft dune and within an hour thirteen children (seven girls and six boys) were 'extending', so they said. ... The assignment of space was organised and the furnishing elaborate.[17]

These scenes are powerful not simply because they provide a critique of psychology's means of claim-making, but because they capture the world-making force of children and their play at the height of the apartheid machinery's abuse. They offer a picture of "learning" that is not merely emulation or the logical application of criteria by means of rational experiment.[18] The scenes of instruction emerging from the sandy dunes of Crossroads contrast subtly with those reflected on by the young men in *War in Worcester*, whose adolescence not far from Crossroads was forged in the crucible of police violence during the same period (the early to late 1980s). While Piaget's theories of cognitive development might not be in vogue in anthropology anymore, what remains is a detailed examination of children's creative, emotional, and relational responses to the destruction of ordinary life under apartheid.

The research in Crossroads marked the beginning of an argument about the importance of "consider[ing] the lot of children whose lives have been disrupted, uprooted, shredded by an evil system."[19] In South Africa, "there is need for much more work on excavating the reality of children's experience. We ought to know what the real impacts of discrimination, migration, re-location and repatriation are on children."[20] As she concludes, "It is easy to sentimentalise childhood. It is easy to summarise in glib generalisations children's experiences. It is difficult to record these experiences in detail and in relation to a socio-historical moment."[21]

Here is the pedagogical heart of the matter: the intellectual and ethical effort to train attention on that which is structurally invisible and profoundly at stake is not merely an expression of liberal concern with childhood as a precious or sentimental affair, but is a central concern of society and its reproduction, as a growing tradition in anthropology has shown (from Margaret Mead to Robert LeVine, David Lancy, and Alcinda Honwana). Not only is the category of the child brought into view but equally apartheid as a system that thoroughly disrupted social reproduction at a minute level. It is a disruption that comes into focus partly by means of a reciprocal assertion of humanity in the face of oppression, and it is in the force of such a reciprocating gesture that protean forms of conscience are contained:

> The book documents the impact that apartheid has on each child's life - it records that their families are forced to build shacks on the sand; that their shacks are demolished before their eyes; that their parents are imprisoned for being in white man's territory; that their education is grossly inadequate; that their mobility and opportunities are rigidly confined.

Those facets of the children's lives are visible and relatively easily measured and recorded. The book does more. It documents the impact of the system on the children's fantasies, dreams and play.[22]

The methodological import is thus demonstrated in the ways links are traced between child thought and the states of consciousness represented in adults' formulations about society: "There is no one consciousness to which adults introduce children."[23]

In 1980, I was three years old and being raised by political-exile parents on a Farm School for Appropriate Technology in Swaziland. Around that time, I remember a friend of my parents, an underground MK soldier[24], joking about being a racist, and I imagined he was talking about being a racing cyclist. I remember the story of Petrus and Jabulile Nyawose, whose daughter was in the class my mother taught at Malkerns Valley Primary School, who were killed by a car bomb in 1982 sent by the apartheid police. After we moved to post-independence Zimbabwe in 1983, my mother suffered PTSD-like flashbacks of interrogation in detention in 1972. I remember the car bomb at the Avondale Shops and more MK visitors to our house during the 1980s. By age eight, I knew all the bare facts of apartheid and the South African struggle, the reasons for celebrating Zimbabwe's independence in 1980, and our place in these historical events. I cannot say I understood them until much later. It is this delay or hesitation or aspect blindness that I am now interested in: what is it about a social or political context that predicts a particular outlook or sensibility? In being introduced to an economy of pain, here in its most political aspect, what does it mean not to submit to an assumption about how one is inserted into that economy? As Cavell notes on the constitutive difficulty of maintaining a distinction between the words expressing pain and the pain itself: "I do not mean to say that the imagination can never be fired by information, rather that you cannot always know when the fire will strike."[25]

It is here that the question of bequest and the picture of learning the grammar of a world begins to come into focus. In my own fieldwork with timber plantation labourers in KwaZulu-Natal in 2009-10, I tried to capture something of the force of world-making play amongst children.

Projecting worlds: notes from a doctoral dissertation, "Labour, Life, and Love in the Timber Plantations of KwaZulu-Natal, South Africa"

Towards the end of my fieldwork in February 2010, I began asking the timber plantation workers that I had come to know about the physical organization of their homesteads because the diversity of each of their residences signalled something of the fragments and transformations I was beginning to see in the landscape at large. It was while talking to Nobuhle about her family's homestead and its spatial layout, hearing about who planted the mango trees and the rationale for the arrangement of rooms around the yard, the flat-roofed squares and the thatched rounds, that her daughter Ntombi called for our attention to show us the map she had drawn in her school exercise book.

Too shy to explain the map, all Ntombi would say as she proudly opened her exercise book was that she had drawn it for her teacher at school. In blue ballpoint pen, across two pages, the world was charted. In the centre lies Gazilini, its rural character marked by trees, round huts and *igqukwane*, the small woven shelters dedicated to the shades. There is no obvious point from which to start one's journey, but snaking roads lead from the skyscrapers and beach resorts of Durban's North Beach, through white and wealthy Umhlanga Rocks, north to the market towns of Zululand, and then to the "rural area" amidst the trees. Another branch of roads leads through the former homelands, through rows of matchbox houses to the towering apartment blocks of Johannesburg. At each junction sits a taxi rank or a bus stop; each locale has distinct housing types; the roads are either tarred and painted or empty and unpaved. Hospitals, schools, clinics, hostels, hotels, even erosion, are carefully marked. The sprawling township of Umlazi, the urban periphery of Durban famous for its migrant labourers' hostels, cosmopolitan mixing, and sheer size, is dislocated here. In this map it lies beyond the city, tucked in to the "rural area" of the upper left corner. In fact, the map rearranges rural and urban into alternative proximities, each indexed by housing type and environmental feature (such as trees or "erosion"). In my photograph of Ntombi's map, I've captured her fingers on the edges holding it up.

In this neat drawing, a network of intensities emerges that hints at what Deleuze calls, in "What Children Say", a "dynamic trajectory."[26] The routes and worlds hinted at in this drawing dislodge the panoptic and synoptic conventions of cartography and make uncertain the location of the drawer, the reader, the traveller, or the production of the map itself. Although these are not quite Lewin's hodological spaces "with their routes, their detours, their barriers, their agents,"[27] the figurations of desire are clear: the revolving restaurant on the John Ross building in Durban, or the township near "Johannesburg" which she has labelled "empilenhle"[28] (does

50

she mean 'good health'? 'the good life'? Towards or at the place of the good life?). I take this map to indicate the presence of alternative geographies, and of the imaginative possibilities of being otherwise. When Deleuze says, "It is the libido's business to haunt history and geography, to organize formations of worlds and constellations of universes, to make continents drift and to populate them with races, tribes, and nations,"[29] I take him to be pointing to the ways in which desire, anticipation and possibility upend disciplines and conventions of knowledge, and forge new trajectories for being otherwise.

And the underneath of this map, its double, is right there on the ground beneath it. Ntombi and her sister have been avoiding their younger brother and his friend who have been playing under the mango tree in the corner of the yard. The two boys have been making their own world out of mud and at our excitement at the girl's map, they draw us to their own creation. Not written on paper produced by the sweat of their mothers' labour, this is the ground itself. A road has been scraped in the earth from the centre of the yard to the private space behind the mango tree, and in the corner, out of the detritus of rural life, is a detailed scene of domesticity: cars, bedrooms, kitchens, stoves, lounges, and all the fine accoutrements of everyday life provided by re-purposed batteries, staplers, medicine boxes, cell phones, circuit boards and sponges. It is an exploded view from above that allows an intimate look at the micro-details of domestic space. Tiny pieces of chopped guava cook on a two-plate electric stove made from bottle tops.[30] A toy car is parked in its garage with a trailer cut from the bottom of a box of sour milk. Thinly insulated telephone wires connect the bottle-top stoves in the kitchen, where the top of a lotion dispenser provides a water tap, to the bedroom where a sponge makes a foam mattress. A carpet accompanies the bed and a table fashioned from an old light fitting with one tiny candelabrum still intact. The remains of a car tape player give the room a hi-fi system and an empty box of Vicks cough syrup provides a cupboard. The pinched mud walls, cleared roads and upright sticks for a gateway that mark out the cleared space of the miniature yard-within-a-yard express a disconcerting accuracy of observation. The creative repurposing of discarded and broken objects into the material for a complete scene of domestic construction is uncanny in its approximations and correspondences.

The Zikhali homestead, nestled in the bend of the Nyalazi River as it curves along the perimeter of the plantations, is surrounded by newly planted stands of sugar cane and eucalyptus, the private investments of local "out growers" who have gained permission from the *induna* (customary authority) to use communal land for commercial agriculture. However, these two maps, on paper and on the ground, suggest a different emplotment of Zikhali domesticity and genealogical relations that exceed the cartographic, statistical and epidemiological techniques brought to bear on them. Thus the bonds that tie together spatialized notions of the yard (Zikhali), the local area (Mfekayi), the plantation (Nyalazi), the municipality (uMkhanyekude), the district (Hlabisa) and the province (KwaZulu-Natal) — and the names attached to those concepts — are loosened by these creative gestures. The girls draw the open highway and big city in an exercise book from school. The boys build from earth and discarded micro-objects. Making use of available materials and gestures — lined paper, schooled habits of drawing, discarded objects

52

and the earth itself — the children's maps show how the life worlds of timber plantation labourers and their families both absorb the presuppositions and entailments of cartography, and break them open to forge creative alternatives.

While I did not look closely at children's play around the plantations, I described a "game" that women play in the plantations called *umshado wokudlala*, or playful marriage. While it seemed that it was precisely its "non-serious" qualities that allowed the seriousness of the game to proceed unnoticed by men and the opening of possibilities that the game achieved, I was struck by the inadequacy of functional explanations of the concept of "play" that appeared in related literature. In my attempt to understand and describe the labour regime of the timber plantations in post-apartheid South Africa of 2010, the pressure of a history of legalised oppression and dislocation seemed obvious, and the world-making efforts of the women who toiled in the plantations no less precarious.

Traditional Healers and Childhood in Zimbabwe

Zimbabwe's independence from white colonial rule came in 1980 after a long and bloody bush war that ended almost a hundred years of colonial domination. In 1982-83, Pamela conducted fieldwork with sixty traditional healers (*n'angas* in Zezuru) in Mashonaland province, to find out about conceptions of childhood and patterns of learning among healers. *Traditional Healers and Childhood in Zimbabwe* examines the precepts in the Zezuru system of healing that describe conceptions of childhood, and it describes healers' understanding of the place of children in cosmology, their relationships with the supernatural and with their clients, including children. In particular, the book explores what conceptions of childhood inform healers' treatment of children; their acquisition of knowledge and its transmission across the generations.[31]

The book is remarkable in drawing the reader's attention to the vital work of healers in reconstituting the conditions of possibility for living together in community in the aftermath of the war.[32] "Communities were licking their wounds and re-erecting the scaffolding of relations to support the ordinary rounds of daily life."[33] Without attempting to be a *complete* ethnography in the traditional style of anthropology, Pamela offers a "partial ethnography", "fragments that suggest ways of seeing childhood in Africa,"[34] in order to invite "more subtle, concrete ways of reading and writing about childhood in southern Africa."[35] The particulars are rich and detailed, and the insight penetrating:

> It seemed to me that in the early 1980s healers were participating in a reflexive moral self-critique. They were examining the past and the character of idealised social categories and in so doing gave flexibility to the present. It was a fascinating process: undertaken in a quiet, understated way, yet the moral issues explored were of momentous importance in the lives of individuals and of social groups. The issues included guilt, pain, trauma, confession, evil, witchcraft, trust, ambition, culpability, hierarchy, and possession. I sought to describe their expression as they reflected on the social categories used to describe childhood.[36]

Reynolds describes in great detail the process of acquiring knowledge, both normatively and in case studies. Here one can glean a sense of the intricate process through which healing as skill and knowledge is encoded in Zezuru life. In childhood: "A healer *may* be selected by a spirit in childhood. Signs of calling in early childhood add authenticity to claims of healing ability... Special ties are established between a child and a healer, often between grandparent and grandchild... The *instruction* is enlarged on from the age of nine."[37] In young adulthood: "At about the age of thirteen, the child begins to collect herbs and prepare medicines along.... The process of 'matriculation' begins, characterised by illness and dreams... the next stage is actual possession... Soon thereafter the healer begins to treat in his own right ... Patients are often referred to senior healers until the spirit reveals the means to treat a wider spectrum of problems. The senior healer often does not charge the patients thus referred and informs the junior healer of the diagnosis and treatment. And so the process of learning continues."[38] In middle age: "the healer reaches the peak of her career in middle age... During the process of drawing out spirits, the aspirants share their dreams of herbs with the senior leader who collects them and uses them in treatment. Again there is the opportunity to exchange knowledge."[39] In old age: "Finally, the healer becomes old and the ambivalence in his status becomes exaggerated. He is widely respected, yet people suspect that his powers are declining... Convention holds that the leader is not expected to pass on his knowledge except as a shade, once dead. However, substantial evidence indicates that grandchildren are trained to assume the healing role after the healer's death.[40] Death: "Death is followed by the eventual possession of a kin member by the healer's spirit, often after a period of intense rivalry within the family.... Kin play an influential part in the emergence of the healers."[41]

There are many aching accounts of witness, involvement, and suffering through the years of the bush war in which Rhodesian and guerrilla forces fought with and through civilian communities. The work demonstrates the beginning of a focus on morality, ethics, conscience and comportment - not in terms of the social context, as perhaps in *Childhood in Crossroads*, but in lives and forms of living. The frame is that of life after war, and the opportunities for healing children's suffering through ritual, where many forms of complicity and pain bound people together in awful ways: "Immediately after the war Gororo treated many cases of young boys with guilty consciences (*zviito zvavakaita*)… Perhaps we need to stress that the possibility exists for ritual specialists to create order and stir disorder… During the war in Zimbabwe, in the Musami area, children as young as twelve became messengers between the guerrillas, hiding in the hills, and the villagers and they gained power even over the lives of persons they reported to the guerrillas as being sell-outs…."[42]

Healers thus played a crucial role in stitching together the conditions of possibility for communities to live together after the war ended in 1980. "In responding to post-war conditions they were creative, flexible, and caring in a way that demonstrates their integrity within communities. … Whatever the nature of a child's problem, he or she can claim the attention of society's specialists and can be directly involved in society's ritual means of curing, explaining, and comforting. … I was deeply impressed by the commitment and concern of healers in their handling of troubled children."[43]

Children and healers together offer a picture of inheritance that bends the meaning of trauma and suggests that learning is less cognitive than it is mediated by a host of social processes and institutions: "...as Bachelard phrased it, 'mediated childhood is more than the sum of our memories.'"[44] Inheritance and healers' enfolding of children offer a different poetics of healing. Conscience is an inadequate name for this poetics, but it strikes closer than ethics or "the ethical". I mean it to run the seam of the question of learning that ethics doesn't quite touch: "How the expression of evil is interpreted has grave implications for the process of healing. Ideas of guilt, sin, personal culpability, identity, dependence, and destiny are acquired by children and internalised. Therapy that fails to place illness within the context of cosmology loses efficacy. A person is a tree that can be shaken at any time."[45]

The Zambezi Valley

From 1984, Pamela conducted fieldwork in the Zambezi Valley with Tonga people after the inundation and destruction of their homes in the building of Lake Kariba. Two books and many articles emerged from that work, including *Lwaano Lwankyika: Tonga Book of the Earth* and *Dance Civet Cat*. The latter was a "description of children's work in the context of subsistence agriculture,"[46] an experiment (as she describes it) with method as it applies to both the study of children and agricultural labour, placing children in the centre of an analysis of broader social, economic, and political forces.[47] *Dance Civet Cat* has five aims, which indicates the layered thinking in the text (I keep to her words closely here): (1) to discover whether children work, how much, of what value their work is to society, what constraints work places on their opportunities, and how it fosters growth and the accumulation of knowledge; (2) to consider social differentiation, in particular with the impact of stages in the life cycle and the distinction drawn by age and gender; (3) to consider the individual as a social agent using strategies, silences, relationships; (4) to consider method - the recording of facts and the tracing of routine; and (5) the study reflects on the nature of knowledge.[48]

The innovative techniques developed to capture the routines and labours of the young provide an exhaustive account of intricate webs through which children are held in Tonga society. Two key events condition the question of child labour here: the inundation of the valley to form Lake Kariba in the 1950s; and independence from white rule in 1980. One was proximate in space, the other in time. Together they frame the ways in which livelihood depended crucially on the young, and the stakes of social change in the early 1980s on the periphery of a postcolonial frontline state. In this fine-grained description food security, surplus labour, and children's rights are voguish concepts that suffer the scrutiny that ethnographic detail provides. "An approach through child work and this to the mother's and father's and that of kin in relation to children's rights, needs, safety, training and opportunities may tease out some of the processes more clearly."[49]

This ethnography has many exemplary features, but what stands out for me is the fine attention paid to labour that is almost impossible to measure or record, in particular the work of young boys to secure kinship relations of care and patronage. The wealth of detail on fields, hours, crops, water fetching etc. that involves mostly girls, highlights the immeasurable value of another kind of labour performed by young boys.

In 1984 and 1985 four of the 24 children – Gweda, Nkombo, Paizon and Gobwi – had no male kinsmen attending to their security at home. This was obvious in the poverty of their diet and their clothing, and in the trouble they had trying to find money for school fees and uniforms. Two of them dropped out of school. Their insecurity may be temporary given the society's mobility in marriage and residence, but the impact on a particular child of relative insecurity can be profound. The children took advantage of different strategies according to their sex. Paizon, for example, spent most of his hours out of school nurturing patron-client ties with male kinsmen some ten years older than he.[50]

Paizon's diaries detail the amount of time he devotes to the nurturance of these relationships; he does not, of course, label them as I have done. It is worth noting that the quality of these relationships (including their motive force and their productiveness) elude the techniques used to record labour described in Chapter Two. Paizon, according to these techniques, spent the least amount of time of all the children working. Yet he and his family were supported largely by the kinsmen with whom Paizon had established particular relationships. Through gifts to him and through the sale of poultry raised from birds given to him the family was able to purchase food in 1984, the third successive year of drought. Paizon's 'work' is of a sociopolitical nature that exploits kinship norms of care and support: work that is very difficult to record yet no less important for that.[51]

There are many such moments where the intimacy of kinship and products of labour are stitched through an ethic: "Boys are expected to build a house for themselves once they turn 10 or 12. The building marks a boy's growth into manhood. Often father helps, teaches and guides the construction. Father and son take pride in each other."[52]

My mother worked with Pamela on producing a book for the children of the Gwembe Tonga called *Lwaano Lwanyika*,[53] which was intended as a resource for future generations of Tonga. I remember hearing tales of art classes and libraries with and for these children, and Rhodesian game rangers and wild animals tearing through hosts' veggie gardens. I got to know Pamela's children well during the time that our mothers were away for several weeks at a time while compiling this book. I also remember the excitement of visiting the new Sheraton hotel in Harare with thousands of school children from around the city to hear President Mugabe address the Front Line States conference in the late 1980s. Later I came to think of that period as intensely meaningful, in political terms, as somehow important in making sense of my own life.

Inheriting War in Worcester

My family "returned" to South Africa in January 1991 at the same time that Pamela's family relocated to South Africa. It was a risky time during the CODESA negotiations that preceded the 1994 elections, and the Truth and Reconciliation Commission (TRC) that came afterwards. I began undergraduate studies in social anthropology in 1995 at the University of Cape Town, where Pamela taught from 1991 to 1999. I remember having to learn, from 1991, the meaning of "race" in South Africa, and reeling at the violence under the surface of everyday life. In 1996, Pamela and Fiona Ross began a study of the TRC, the project captured in *War in Worcester*, which tracked the Human Rights Violations hearings, reflecting, amongst other things, on the ethical reach of the young in the Commission's deliberations. After some time, they included in their project young activists who fought against apartheid in Zwelethemba, a suburb of Worcester, a hundred kilometres north of Cape Town. Pamela worked with a group of fourteen men who had been young anti-apartheid activists during the 1980s, and each of whom was a member of the ANC in whose name they had acted, and Fiona worked with a group of women[54] who had operated alongside the men in fighting against the state. I remember as an Honours student, accompanying Pamela, Fiona, Susan Levine, and Patti Henderson, with their interlocutors and collaborators, to Zwelathemba, in Worcester, where we learned about community surveys, transects, and testimonies and where we completed small studies related to the main project.

War in Worcester examines the TRC through the role the young played in securing the end of oppression. Reynolds sought to learn about young activists' commitment over time, their political consciousness, their development, their ethics, their actions, and the consequences of their involvement, amongst other things. What emerges is not simply that the TRC was not systematic in its attempt to include a record of the young as activists, or that the categories it used of victim and perpetrator were misleading and harmful, or that a high price was paid, and is being paid individually and collectively, for those omissions. Apart from a critique of the Commission's work, what is striking are the complex moral and ethical grounds on which politics and self were forged in the intensity of a war that remains unacknowledged by public discourse on "the struggle". In considering the delicate balance that young activists tried to achieve between

61

disobeying parents and objecting vehemently to an unjust government as well as carving out care and concern for comrades in the midst of annihilating torture and incarceration, description itself is challenged: "The question is, of course: what is description? Is it a chronicle or a product of reflection? Under what circumstances, in what place, across what span of time, before whom is it made? ... Any description of major conflicts has an elliptical relationship to what actually happened."[55]

Pamela cites Veena Das's observations that "the most compelling moments for her in ethnography have occurred when she found someone responding to events that put his or her entire life into question... [Das] observes that 'there is something resistant to thought when we try and imagine the condition of being wounded ... something else than rational argument is called for in the face of this condition - not simply emotion or empathy but "wakefulness to one's 'life'"'. In Zwelethemba, the scene was a request to remember... In the process of our meetings, the men seemed to be engaged in a retrieval of the condition of being wounded, so that a certain balance of reason and emotion could be achieved in the service of remembering."[56] Such insight resonates with Alphonso Lingis' notion of "violations" as necessary and constitutive of the possibility for relations with others, and thus for thinking and feeling.[57]

Consider here the mediations of such vulnerability and such wounds, not in the recollections of Pamela's collaborators, but in the anthropologist's gloss that situates the reader, writer, and implied speakers in a concatenating line of presuppositions and entailments:

We spoke, for example, often glancingly, about heroism and cowardice and how difficult it had been to hold onto a sense of pride or virtue after torture or after having experienced the clever, invasive forms of humiliation at which the security force members excelled. The men did not speak in romantic terms about the past, though there had been heady days, nor with much nostalgia, except sometimes for comradeship shared, leadership exercised, and direction assured.[58]

In July 2016, I re-read *War in Worcester* with a class of ten postgraduate students at Stellenbosch University, alongside recent literature on "ordinary ethics". The class was bookended on the one hand by the 2015 student protests across South Africa, of which the Stellenbosch activism had been a crucial part, with its own valences and particularities, and on the other by the looming funding crisis besetting universities and the fulfillment of a promise of further protests in the second half of 2016. A number of anthropology students had taken up leadership positions in the various movements, while others were critical, skeptical, or hostile to their demands. I was curious to see what readings of *War in Worcester* might emerge from this context.

Many of the students were struck silent by the horrific details of state violence meted out on the bodies of the young. There was no doubt as to the sense of horror provoked by the accounts given of the young men whose lives were geographically proximate to the students (Worcester is 90 kilometers from Stellenbosch and on the same range of mountains); the difficulty was in finding the appropriate temporal frame in which to receive this knowledge. Ordinary and extraordinary, as modes of ethical life, struggled to travel beyond the limits of "apartheid" as a distant, historical thing. How did it relate to the campus struggles of 2015 and the unfolding battles of 2016?[59] My own efforts to sketch out a question of ethical concern, of the reach and limits of activism, of the sense and sensibility of student action, seemed to fall flat, or at least I struggled to gauge the class's response.

Lovelyn Nwadeyi was one of the leaders to emerge from the #FeesMustFall activism at Stellenbosch, and one who has given voice to the ethical and political urgency of the student movements. In a celebrated speech to Stellenbosch's Convocation in January 2016 ("Courage, Compassion and Complexity: Reflections on the new Matieland and South Africa"[60]), she spoke eloquently about the difficulty of affording dignity and respect through modes of address across languages in the light of the terrible histories of racialized violence that Stellenbosch still signifies. The TRC, along with "rainbowism" and "Mandela's sell out" are prominent objects of critique for young students across the country. As Nwadeyi said that night referring to the activist students, "We have created no room for capitalists without conscience, no room for patriarchs, racists, homophobes, ageists or able-ists. The inappropriately labelled born frees are saying that we will employ an intersectional feminism that squarely confronts a system of oppression that neither the TRC nor the current South African constitution has been able to sufficiently address". She went on to say that, "We have a choice as South Africans to reclaim our humanity; both apartheid and colonisation dehumanised us all by giving white people a superiority complex and black people an inferiority complex, albeit with different consequences. We were all dehumanised and we must dismantle this inhumanity that we are all products of by reclaiming our collective humanity. We must reclaim our histories so that both our children will know exactly the truth about themselves. We must reclaim our languages so that those who choose to speak our languages do so out of pure love, like I speak Afrikaans, and not out of obligation. I look forward to the day when I do not have to talk to my children about racism. That is really my dream for South Africa ..."[61]

Conclusion

be in your world, but perhaps not of your flesh...[62]

While Lovelyn spoke confidently of love and the need to reclaim humanity, Pamela's work suggests that a standing language for such a project must be both more tenuous and more profound than the current crisis has acknowledged. More than just a question of making oneself known to oneself - and of being known by another - is the challenge of learning how to articulate the crisis one finds oneself in; of discerning what must be rejected and what continued, with what consequence. Here I am thinking both in relation to the broader sense of crisis for the young in South Africa, only part of which is captured by vocal students on university campuses; and in relation to an initiation into anthropology. Here I return finally to Cavell's notion of "availability"[63] and the possibility of mutual attunement. I have tried to suggest that Pamela's work provides a picture of that availability in densely ethnographic terms; and a means by which to think how we might come into relation with another, in the midst of such terrible colonial trauma and revolutionary violence. I cannot think counterfactually for all of anthropology in any context; most concretely I am thinking from this context, but I must imagine other scenes in which such a picture of bequest becomes relevant.

As Cavell says of the learning of new words in new contexts: "new needs, new relationships, new objects, new perceptions to be recorded and shared...the 'routes of initiation' are never closed."[64] The standing threat that my students will learn nothing from my gestures and words, as perhaps I might have learned nothing from my teachers, is part of the "fierce ambiguity" not only of (learning a) language but anthropology. "But perhaps we are too quick to suppose we know what it is in such situations that makes us say the child is learning something. In particular, too quick to suppose we know what the child is learning. To say we are teaching them language obscures both how different what they learn may be from anything we think we are teaching, or mean to be teaching; and how vastly more they learn than the thing we should say we had 'taught'. Different and more, not because we are bad or good teachers, but because 'learning' is not as academic a matter as academics are apt to suppose."[65]

Rather than arrive at a picture of anthropologists and their interlocutors waving and mouthing in each other's direction but wholly alone and misguided in their knowledge of each other, I want to suggest that Pamela's work provides a thickly enfleshed means by which to see how words and gestures, during and after politics and violence, might allow us to navigate a route towards the sharing of flesh. The extent of the theft of the student, or the desire of the child to speak that must exceed her capacity, remains in question; or rather remains my own question.[66]

Notes

[1] Stanley Cavell, *The Claim of Reason* (Cambridge: Oxford University Press, 1979), 198.

[2] Marshall Sahlin's recent argument concerning kinship provides a language for that quality of relatedness in which we have a deep stake in one another, but I do not agree with all of what he says there. See *What Kinship Is-And is Not* (Chicago: University of Chicago Press, 2013).

[3] Cavell, *The Claim of Reason*, 189.

[4] *Ibid.*

[5] *Ibid.*

[6] João Biehl, "Ethnography in the Way of Theory," *Cultural Anthropology* 28 (2013): 573-597.

[7] Pamela Reynolds, *Traditional healers and childhood in Zimbabwe* (Athens, OH: Ohio University Press, 1996), 15.

[8] Pamela Reynolds, *War in Worchester: Youth and the Apartheid State* (New York: Fordham University Press, 2013), 140.

[9] Reynolds, *War in Worchester*, 138.

[10] Reynolds, *War in Worchester* 144.

[11] Reynolds, *War in Worchester*, 153.

[12] See Paola Marrati and Todd Meyers, "Life, as Such," introduction to Georges Canguilhem's *Knowledge of Life* (New York: Fordham University Press, 2008).

[13] Pamela Reynolds, *Childhood in Crossroads* (Cape Town: David Philip, 1989), 9.

[14] Reynolds, *Childhood in Crossroads*, 49-50.

[15] Reynolds, *Childhood in Crossroads*, 53.

[16] Reynolds, *Childhood in Crossroads*, 55.

[17] Reynolds, *Childhood in Crossroads*, 57.

[18] Cavell, *The Claim of Reason*.

[19] Reynolds, *Childhood in Crossroads*, 199.

20 Reynolds, *Childhood in Crossroads*, 201.

21 Reynolds, *Childhood in Crossroads*, 199.

22 Reynolds, *Childhood in Crossroads*, 199.

23 Reynolds, *Childhood in Crossroads*, 200.

24 Umkhonto weSizwe, the "Spear of the Nation," was the armed wing of the African National Congress, co-founded by Nelson Mandela in the wake of the Sharpeville massacre.

25 Cavell, *The Claim of Reason*, 338.

26 Gilles Deleuze, *Essays Clinical and Critical* (London: Verso, 1998), 61.

27 *Ibid.*

28 In isiZulu, *mpilo* is translated as health or life; *nhle* as good. Here it is in the locative form used for indicating place or direction.

29 Deleuze, *Essays Clinical and Critical*, 62.

30 While this might look like play, in Piaget's sense, found in *Play, Dreams and Imitation in Childhood* (Routledge, 1951), I argue against this picture of play as developmentalism in the figure of the child.

31 Reynolds, *Traditional healers and childhood in Zimbabwe*, xiv.

32 See David Lan's *Guns and Rain: Guerrillas and Spirit Mediums in Zimbabwe* (Berkeley: University of California Press, 1985).

33 Reynolds, *Traditional healers and childhood in Zimbabwe*, xvii.

34 Reynolds, *Traditional healers and childhood in Zimbabwe*, xxxiv.

35 Reynolds, *Traditional healers and childhood in Zimbabwe*, xxiii.

36 Reynolds, *Traditional healers and childhood in Zimbabwe*, xxix.

37 Reynolds, *Traditional healers and childhood in Zimbabwe*, 6-7, original emphasis.

38 Reynolds, *Traditional healers and childhood in Zimbabwe*, 7-8.

39 Reynolds, *Traditional healers and childhood in Zimbabwe*, 8.

40 Reynolds, *Traditional healers and childhood in Zimbabwe*, 9.

41 *Ibid.*

42 Reynolds, *Traditional healers and childhood in Zimbabwe*, 67.

[43] *Ibid.*

[44] Gaston Bachelard, *The Poetics of Reverie: Childhood, Language, and the Cosmos* (New York: Beacon, 1971), 126, in Reynolds, *Traditional healers and childhood in Zimbabwe*, 34.

[45] Reynolds, *Traditional healers and childhood in Zimbabwe*, 94.

[46] Pamela Reynolds, *Dance Civet Cat* (London: Zed Books, 1991), xix.

[47] *Ibid.*

[48] Reynolds, *Dance Civet Cat*, xix.

[49] Reynolds, *Dance Civet Cat*, xxvii.

[50] Reynolds, *Dance Civet Cat*, 137.

[51] Reynolds, *Dance Civet Cat*, 140.

[52] Reynolds, *Childhood in Crossroads*, 128.

[53] Pamela Reynolds and Colleen Crawford Cousins, *Lwaano Lwanyika, The Tonga*

Book of the Earth (London: Panos, 1994).

[54] Fiona Ross, *Bearing Witness: Women and the Truth and Reconciliation Commission* (Pluto, 2003).

[55] Reynolds, *War in Worcester*, 3.

[56] Reynolds, *War in Worcester*, 4.

[57] Alphonso Lingis, *Dangerous Emotions* (Berkeley: University of California Press, 2000), 85.

[58] Reynolds, *War in Worcester*, 22.

[59] See WISER Salon Vol 9, 2015, http://jwtc.org.za/the_salon/volume_9.htm and http://www.litnet.co.za/interview-with-achille-mbembe/ Accessed: July 7, 2017.

[60] Video of speech found at https://www.youtube.com/watch?v=JqaZVH7cUJo Accessed: July 7, 2017.

[61] *Ibid.*

[62] Cavell, *The Claim of Reason*, 189.

[63] Stanley Cavell, "The Availability of Wittgenstein's Later Philosophy," *Philosophical Review* 71 (1962): 67–93

[64] Cavell, *The Claim of Reason*, 180.

[65] Cavell, *The Claim of Reason*, 171.

[66] "Such uses have consequences in the kind of understanding and communication they make possible. I want to say: It is such shades of sense, intimations of meaning, which allow certain kinds of subtlety or delicacy of communication; the connection is intimate, but fragile. Persons who cannot use words, or gestures, in these ways with you may yet be in your world, but perhaps not of your flesh. The phenomenon I am calling 'projecting a world' is the fact of language which, I take it, is sometimes responded to by saying that 'All language is metaphorical'. Perhaps one could say: the possibility of metaphor is the same as the possibility of language generally, but what is essential to the projection of a word is that it proceeds, or can be made to proceed, naturally; what is essential to a functioning metaphor is that its 'transfer' is unnatural — it breaks up the established, normal directions of projection." Cavell, *The Claim of Reason*, 190.

4

The Ungovernable and Dangerous
Children, sexuality, and anthropology

Vaibhav Saria

Introduction

My research interest in the HIV epidemic predated my
training in Anthropology.[1] It was sparked by graffiti painted
on a wall next to one of the many busy traffic intersections in
Calcutta. The year was 1995 and I was around 9 years old.
The graffiti depicted an exaggerated limp wrist, attached to a
man against a green background, and read, "Queenies are not
the only ones who get AIDS". It was the first depiction I had
ever come across of somebody like me. At the time, I was
being mercilessly teased and tormented by everybody for
being effeminate, and in a way encountering that image
shattered my isolation. I welcomed the company of that
cartoonish image, painted not as part of any artistic endeavor
but to serve a more functional purpose: to dispel
misinformation about HIV transmission. I had enough
intelligence at that age to understand the implication that
"queenies got AIDS."

Though this was my first encounter with the queenie, it
wasn't my first encounter with AIDS. A few months before
clapping eyes on the queenie, I had seen a photograph in the
local newspaper that showed a lot of young children, younger
than I was at that time, wearing signs around their necks that
said 'AIDS'. Some were wearing signs that said 'HIV+'. My
brother and I were both curious and he had asked our tutor

what it meant. Our tutor said, "I don't know"; my brother persisted by saying, "It was in today's newspaper" and I joined in to describe this photograph. Our tutor shook her head and started correcting our exercises with a foreboding expression that shut us up. Fifteen years later, during my doctoral research, I made an educated guess that the photograph was documenting children under state protection who had tested positive for HIV and the state was segregating them into a separate orphanage. The graffiti has since been long removed but was an early sign of what was to become of the HIV epidemic juggernaut in India as it was already elsewhere in the world. After more than twenty years, I am still pursuing questions regarding sexuality and HIV; in other words why queenies get AIDS, and my hunt for answers is also my exploration of anthropology.

I start with these autobiographical snippets so as to begin a discussion on the sexuality of children that I hope will show how anthropology allows us to pose questions differently than other disciplines. The question of the sexuality of children is an important part of the discussion of the HIV epidemic, but more broadly I argue that the question of how children learn their sexuality positions us to interrogate the norms which produce the halcyon pictures of childhood that Pamela Reynolds' work cautions against. Few anthropologists have so relentlessly argued for keeping children and young people in the picture when any aspect of society is being discussed or studied. Fewer still have managed to study childhood without giving way to un-interrogated reactions of trying to save children from putative abuses. Pamela Reynolds' work is exceptional in insisting upon the centrality of children to anthropological study as well as for developing frames that circumvent the salvific impulse. Her corpus helps us understand the complexity of children's lives and participation in the social, which complicate normative pictures of their path to adulthood.

It Takes a Village

The ethnographic observations that follow were collected during fieldwork conducted between 2008 and 2013 in the districts of rural Orissa in eastern India. My primary goal was to study the sexual lives of hijras, one of India's "third-gender" populations, now translated as transgender, who are born intersexed or undergo a ritualized castration (though the importance of these criteria in defining a hijra is often overstated). Hijras are often seen in the Indic imaginary as erotic-ascetics who accrete sacred power to bless auspicious events such as weddings, childbirths, new business ventures; they also beg for alms in trains and other public spaces in exchange for blessings of fertility and prosperity. Their sacred power is also seen as dangerous to the extent that hijras can curse men and women with infertility by exposing their castrated genitalia. They attain this sacral power through stepping away from their patriarchal duties, obligations, and the responsibilities of fathering sons and heading families. Historical and anthropological records indicate that hijras often moved away from their villages and families to join hijra communities located in cities.[2] In light of this literature, my research attempted to understand the puzzling question of why the hijras in rural Orissa had not moved away, but had remained with their natal families. Furthermore, I wondered about how the lack of anonymity, secrecy, and privacy that urban areas offered, intersected with their sexual activities and the erotic economies of rural India. What I had not anticipated, and thus took me by surprise, was the significance of the figure of the child, as well as the role of children, both in the lives of hijras and in the erotic economies of rural India.

The following scene took place one hot summer afternoon early in my fieldwork. Jaina, a hijra in her early 70s then, would often take her afternoon siesta at my residence: a room in the local bangle factory. The door to my room faced a large window with a wrought iron grille. Jaina would sleep in front of the door that was left open for some air to alleviate the suffocating heat. Inevitably, our siestas would be interrupted by a leer of young boys, not yet in their teenage years, who would climb the grille and shout at the sleeping Jaina to wake up and show them her "vagina". Jaina would indulge them, laughingly pick up her sarong, and expose herself to their gaze. I was alarmed by this gesture since the queer subject has so often been vilified as a figure that sexually abuses children that it has prefigured the queer's claims on the liberal state (by disputing the propinquity between queerness and paedophilia).[3] The scene of seduction that was unfolding in my hut came dangerously close to upholding the stereotype of the queer subject as sexually dangerous to children. The appearance of children in this scene was also unexpected, because the queer has often been positioned as outside to the project of the family and kinship, of which the child is emblematic.[4] Their insistence on viewing the feared locus, given that exposure is used as a threat to curse with infertility in other contexts, such as when people do not give money during begging, points to questions of sexual curiosity in children. It is a certain moment of incipience that raises questions that cannot be addressed by taking recourse to inflated notions of children's agency or lack thereof. As I will show, taking an anthropological perspective demonstrates how this encounter can neither be excused through arguments about relativism nor condemned through a universal idea of normative sexuality and childhood. Instead it points us to how ideas of consent, coercion, use, abuse, and violence are taught and learnt in sites where discourses that pathologize children or attraction to them have no currency.

Before proceeding further, let me provide a picture of how the figure of the child was conceived in the sexual landscape of rural Orissa. I was struck by the frequent and banal ways in which adults would use sexual profanities in the presence of children because they would assume that children wouldn't understand them. The adults, including men, women, and the hijras, would not think twice before using sexual terms to describe a person or a situation in front of children of all ages. This would often result in very funny situations. One day Jaina and her nieces were describing how a man who had lent one of the nieces some money was making life difficult by his constant demands for the loan to be repaid with interest. Jaina advised, "Try and return the money as soon as possible otherwise he is going to screw us well." She continued to think and mumble to herself, "What a big fucker he has turned out to be, he is going to screw us all." Her niece who was 7 years old and playing at her feet, suddenly asked, "What is he going to do?" Jaina irritably replied, "Nothing" but the niece persisted and kept on asking, "What is he going to do, tell me?" Jaina screamed at her, "Nothing, get away, you mad girl."

While the niece was not offered any more information regarding what the moneylender would do, the male children of varying degrees of kinship in the village, including fictive kin, were offered partial information right from their birth.

When the hijras used to visit babies to ritualistically bless them in exchange for alms, their reactions to girl babies and boy babies were starkly different from each other. While they blessed the newly born girl child and said excitedly how beautiful she is and was going to become, their chattering and excitement over the boy child was distinctly sexual. All the children often referred to hijras in the village as maternal grandmothers and when the hijras visited the babies, including the ones born within their own families, their joking and playing with the baby in front of the whole family and neighbourhood gathered around would go as following: "My god, what a big cock you have? Are you going to fuck your own grandmother [referring to themselves] with that cock?" Such sexual banter would continue with boys of all ages and young boys, as they grew up, would start responding to this teasing. The hijras would often joke with the young male children who were always about the marketplace running errands, helping out at shops, killing time between meals and games, or skipping school. The hijras would ask, "Can you fuck?" or tease them and say, "You are so small, can you even fuck? Will you fuck me?" The boys would either blush and smile and walk away or make the teasing into a repartee by their replies, "Of course, I will fuck you very hard".

Propriety, comportment, and etiquette taught the children early on who would be willing to provide them with information regarding sex. Another afternoon, which I realized was the only time the children were left unsupervised because the adults would be taking their siestas, two boys around 7-10 years old came to Jaina and said, "We want to go to the hotel near the station." Jaina looked confused and asked, "Why?" The boys replied, "We will also do it." Jaina understood what they meant and laughingly rebuked them,

"What will you do? Do you know what you have to do?" The boys said, "Yes" and Jaina challenged them and said, "Do it then, do it here, with me." The boys unzipped and showed their penises to Jaina who snorted scornfully, "what will happen with that? OK, go now." The boys looking chuffed at testing their masculinity ran away gleefully. Jaina started laughing uncontrollably and said, "Oh these children overhear what the older boys talk about, and look they are so young and they want to do it without knowing anything." Jaina, who also doubled up as a Madam (pimp) would arrange for rooms in a hotel run by one of her old lovers for couples wanting to have sex and for clients of prostitutes for a bit of commission. Her commissions were not large or even of a fixed amount but she did earn a lot of gratitude for the arrangement and for safeguarding of secrets. That is what the children meant when they said they wanted to go to the hotel room.

Adults with whom the discussions of sexuality are taboo were not the only ones who populated the child's world in rural Orissa. I borrow the insight of Pamela Reynolds to look "behind kinship" to show that children are exposed to a lot of sex-talk outside their immediate family and did make sense of it slowly as they grew up.[5] Reynolds developed this insight to look "behind kinship" while studying child labour in the Zambezi Valley, to correct the difference in reports of children's labour made by parents, by children themselves, and in observations of the anthropologist.[6] Reynolds argues for "paring down the family" to write against the child as an object, in order to show that they "actively participate in the struggles of individuals and households to maximize their resources and opportunities under the circumstances in which they find themselves".[7] My description of the relationship between the hijras and the children of the village is an attempt to pare down the family as well to show that children participated and actively explored the sexual landscape.

Known but Overlooked

I pursued my explorations at the Department of Anthropology at Johns Hopkins where Pamela Reynolds was my teacher and alleviated my anxieties in pursing this thread of research. Upon reading my field report, which contained a version of the scenes and data described above, she reminded me that before I turn to notions of sexual use and abuse of children, I must delineate the responsibility of the adults with regards to children's sexuality. She furthermore guided me by enquiring, "Is there an element of equality seen as a possibility when sex is sought or mooted from one seen to be an 'outsider', 'outrider' or 'eccentric' in the social scale? Could a relationship with a hijra offer some terms of equality in the child's eyes that is denied in most other settings?" (*Personal Communication*). I shall use these questions to tentatively offer some critical views on Child Sexual Abuse (CSA) as it is assembled in the Indian public sphere. The discourse of same-sex sexuality in India, scholars have pointed out, does not divide itself according to the hetero/homo binary but according to the axis of penetration/penetrated, at least for men.[8] Indeed, phrases referring to sexually penetrating other men were idiomatic in the use to signify a power dynamic that grafted onto other social divisions. The hijras with their sexual banter with boy children introduced them to the privilege of being the man—they were to be men, who penetrated hijras, rather than be emasculated by being penetrated.[9] The male children would soon learn this as they grew up and hijras offered a way for them to experience that pleasure of mastery and domination which they didn't elsewhere, certainly not in their families. Yet as children they had not learnt that this was a form of playing, a simulation and not the real thing and an interesting dynamic of cruelty developed within this gap. Pamela Reynolds reminds us that children also have a set of entitlements along with vulnerabilities. Similarly, the children in Bhadrak had not yet learnt to not abuse such offers from hijras and would often take liberties; their responses to the teasing and flirting would often slip into becoming quite cruel towards the hijras.

The hijras with their sexual teasing, too, would leave themselves open to being abused by the children. Interactions might begin harmlessly with children realizing that they could sing raunchy Hindi songs to the hijras, which they couldn't sing to anybody else, but this would also transform hijras into somebody that they need not respect. Children would often gather muck from the nearby sewer and throw it at hijras, and follow them around chanting, "maichiya, maichiya" [a derogatory word for hijras]. They would slip into hijras' rooms and steal money and sometimes got carried away in their obnoxious boisterousness and physically assault the hijras by punching them or tearing their clothes. These children were then reprimanded by grown-up men to not be cruel to the hijras with whom they might eventually have a sexual relationship post-puberty. If the hijras were responsible for introducing the boys to the semiotics, significance, and pleasures of penetration, then they also made themselves vulnerable to the careless cruelty of children. This relationship required the interventions of other men of the village to be transformed when the children reached adulthood.

Let me offer one example that reveals the importance of learning sexuality correctly for children in relation to hijras. One evening during the course of fieldwork, I saw a group of men gathered around and scolding a group of boys between the ages of 13–17, some of whom I knew. I had to wait to learn what had happened after the group of grown-up men had been disbanded and the young boys had been sent home with stern warnings and threatened with severe beatings. What had been reported as transpiring was that a group of 16 boys had decided to go and have sex with the mentally ill elderly woman who lived in the Bhadrak railway station having been abandoned there by her untraceable family. This woman, just called *paagal buri* [mad old-woman], was a fixture of the train station, having lived there for years and years, nobody knew since when or for how long, exactly.[10] The first time I met her was when I was waiting for my train with the other hijras to go begging and she spoke to me in Bengali. I thought she knew me and that's why she was speaking to me in Bengali.

> Paagal Buri: How far is the Charampa station?
> VS: [puzzled] This is the Charampa station.
> Paagal Buri: Oh really?
> VS : Yes, where do you want to go?
> Paagal Buri: I was thinking of going to Charampa.
> VS: But this is Charampa.
> Paagal Buri: Oh, how far is the Charampa station from here?

The conversation continued for a few minutes longer till the shopkeeper from the shop nearby took her away. The woman, I learnt later, was taken care of by the various people who worked regularly at the train station: shopkeepers, rickshaw drivers, food sellers, railway officials, sweepers, etc. I was told that she was vulnerable to being periodically raped by drunken men from the nearby neighbourhood and by labourers high on drugs, and those who were travelling through the station. The village elders told me that the young boys had learnt of this possibility of sexual access and had thought it would be a great adventure to take advantage of her vulnerability and incapacity to consent.[11] One of the men of the neighbourhood who sells fruits at the train station got suspicious when he saw the group of boys, all of whom he knew, hanging about at the station for no reason. Upon enquiry and interrogation he found out their plans and brought all of them back to the neighbourhood and informed all the elders of the local *panchayat* [local self-government organization that is legally recognized]. The elders and all the men of the neighbourhood saw fit to educate the boys as to why what they were going to do was wrong—this is the scene that I had seen. The point I am trying to make by offering this story is that young men were taught how to govern their sexuality correctly and hijras were part of this pedagogy. It's not as if ideas of consent, abuse, and sexual violence were absent in rural Orissa and that interactions could only be read retrospectively through legal frameworks in the court of law. Hijras who inhabited this local moral world—by teasing, flirting, and seducing these young men—were teaching them how consent, invitations, limits, and conditions vis-à-vis sexuality should be understood and the young men, on the other hand, were seeking the hijras out as teachers.

The local sexual imaginary that I am attempting to describe was not devoid of vocabularies approaching "abuse", but these notions of abuse were extremely gendered and inscribed within particular understandings of justice. The male child was considered to be abused only when penetrated against his will and that too only when he was considered too young to seek revenge for this violence. Thus if the young person could not understand the semiotics of penetration and that he had to seek revenge for his emasculation, his family would then take recourse to law for the violence. Sexual access to the female body of any age was considered to be abuse if it did not follow the strict rules of marriage. Most sexual abuse in rural Orissa, however, was suffered, excused, and understood as yet another effect of the power differentials of caste, class, and feudalism across age and gender. Thus, accounts and incidents were rarely reported to the police and even then as decades of feminist scholarship in India have shown, great courage is required to carry such cases to the courts of justice, where they are rarely given a fair hearing.[12]

Furthermore, in the recounting of violence incidents from their childhood, the adults in rural Orissa even when registering pain and loss, would also make it a point to recount that they have healed and thus law was not the only way or even necessary for reconciliation. These recountings point to the vast anthropological archive that has documented not only varied ideas of loss, pain, and grief but also the systems and narratives of healing that accommodate them.[13] Thus, a large spectrum of experience of sexuality in one's childhood, even when it is violent and abusive, would not be revealed to us in the legal archive because it would not have reached the court. Relying solely on the cases that do call upon the law to deliver justice for sexual wrongs would imply that the relation between childhood and sexuality is not only one of violence but also that children are evacuated of sexuality, which has instead been filled with trauma, violence and abuse. Pamela Reynolds makes a similar point when critiquing the way the young were con-figured in the Truth and Reconciliation Commission in post-apartheid South Africa. A lot of young people in her ethnography refused to testify not only because they thought the extent of abuse they suffered was not greater than that of many others but also because they had suffered as legitimate enemies of the state and thus did not require any retribution. Thus, the work of anthropology, which Pamela once told me was the hunt for a narrative, is necessary to situate knowledge, or flesh out numbers, that are documented, compiled and studied in other disciplines. [14] She writes, "The TRC tended to hear testimonies about instances of gross human rights violations and it was less successful at eliciting and describing the character of a long-drawn out fight in which young people had to anticipate and endure repeated confrontations, detention and torture." [15] Though I am not speaking of a context of violence wrought by the state but of structural poverty, the failure to understand how young people move in and learn their social milieu results in a similar danger of simplifying what childhood entails. Let me turn to one instance where ignoring anthropological knowledge has resulted in legislation that has made children more vulnerable by erasing their sexuality completely.

The Strange Child of Law

The Parliament of India passed the Protection of Children from Sexual Offences Act (POCSO) in 2012 in an attempt to provide harsher penalization of sexual abuse against children. Children were defined as anybody below the age of 18, irrespective of their gender. This act came into fruition after decades of work by child rights activists and was deemed necessary since the existing laws were not considered capable of handling issues of child sexual abuse for a number of reasons. Previously, abuse against children was booked under the sections of 375, 354, and 377 of the Indian Penal Code (IPC). The two sections pertaining mostly to girls were section 375 that criminalized rape and section 354 that criminalized acts that were defined widely by the phrase "outraging the modesty of a woman." Pratiksha Baxi has offered painstaking analysis on how these sections made women more vulnerable in several ways. The most scandalous of these is the way that officials seek evidence of penetration by verifying the damage to the hymen. The absence of the hymen or physiological signs of force and violence is then later used in the court to question and dispute the girl/woman's claim of being raped. Her voice and her body are pitted against each other; her claims for justice are countered by the fact that her body does not show signs of violation. Irrespective of age, the woman's body, in the absence of clear signs of violence, is interpreted freely by the law to render consent to the sexual encounter in question and her voice is then seen as lying and manipulative. [16]

Section 377 of the IPC states that "whoever voluntarily has carnal intercourse against the order of nature with any man, woman, or animal shall be punished with imprisonment for life, or with imprisonment of either description for term which may extend to ten years, and shall also be liable to fine." This section has been used to criminalize homosexuals in India and elsewhere in the commonwealth. The state in India has argued against repealing this section to de-criminalize homosexuality, not because it has taken an active stance against homosexuals but because it is the only law with which persons who rape boys and men through anal penetration can be charged. Activists point out the inadequacy of these sections to deal with cases of child abuse, because they focused solely on the act of peno-vaginal and anal penetration and did not take into account the many ways in which children could be sexually abused. Furthermore, the act rendered any sexual act, consensual or otherwise, with persons below the age of 18 criminal. The addition of this clause shows that by relying on fictions of age rather than the realities of gender, the law erases the different ways in which the gender of the child distributes vulnerabilities; which are usually stacked against the female young person. For example, the law has now tied itself in knots in dealing with the many cases in which the perpetrator of violence was a young man below 18.[17] In one way, POCSO is an attempt to bring social realities into conformity with legal fictions, and to encourage the current climate of moral policing where the law ratifies the policing of sexuality of young people by robbing them of the ability to give consent. The heavy crackdown on young lovers whose affairs transgress case, class, and religious divisions makes such moral policing particularly pernicious.

Laws such as POCSO align themselves toward maintaining a secret of the child's sexuality or an illusion of the innocence of the child that is defined by its ignorance or absence of sexuality. By robbing them of the ability to consent, or rendering them incapable of consenting to sexual acts till the age of 18, POCSO not only hopes to prevent violence and abuse against the children but also correctly govern the traffic of women in marriage and kinship in cases where boundaries of caste, class, religion, and gender are transgressed by young people when one partner might be below 18. Pamela Reynolds, her students, and colleagues have long argued against this assumed innocence.[18] In addition, Aaron Goodfellow shows in his study of gay kinship that "institutional maintenance of secrecy around children's lives is integral to the societal masking of the disciplinary techniques that subjugate desire to the aims of the state and citizenship, or adulthood."[19]

Pamela Reynolds has shown that young people participated in violence in situations where they were fighting the oppression of the state in South Africa. Their participation problematised the characterisations of children and young people as passive victims. Young fighters were neither excluded from forms of reconciliation and reparation, nor were they excused according to Liberation Force rules or in the light of the law for serious breaches in action. Her emphasis on the ethnographic methods of anthropology enables her to show how contradictions are created in the way young people were framed. Children became at once passive victims as well as active perpetrators, a contradiction that excused and explained state violence.[20] Similarly, my ethnographic descriptions are not meant to show that children have the ability to consent to sex, but to argue that they do participate in sexual economies. More specifically, I argue that the veracity of their claims of abuse should not be dependent on whether they have a sexuality or not. Given that children learn the terms, conditions, limits and expressions of sexuality as they progress through the web of sociality, abuse done by them and onto them cannot depend on the biological determination of sexuality. Pamela Reynolds has described the ways in which children's participation in abuse is read as their exposure to evil and witchcraft and the therapeutics offered to them is a way to transition them into adulthood.[21] I wish to take her analysis further and remind us that in all therapeutics there is a margin of failure even for those that claim to cure and heal one of evil and witchcraft; therefore, children may also fail to learn the rules and regulations of sexual conduct.

The scene from the railway station was one such instance where and when the young men failed to act correctly, showing us that young men may not learn proper sexual conduct and may commit violence and abuse, but this should not have implications on how we judge abuse done onto them. Such confusion becomes inevitable when ideas of childhood and children rest on the fulcrum of innocence. Equating the exposure of forms of sexuality with abuse rests on a uniform idea of childhood and innocence, but these ideas come undone when we face cases of sexual abuse that children commit on children. This has led to proliferating sub categories that attempt to categorize the abuse done on and by children such as "Child-on-Child Sexual Abuse", and "Intersibling Abuse" in the discourse of children's sexuality. Further implying that the relationship between childhood and sexuality is not as simple as we would like to believe, and the necessity of anthropological knowledge to understand better when and how reparation can be imagined and measured.

Craft ringing with an armourer's music

> The whole craft ringing
> with an armourer's music
> the course set willfully across
> the ungovernable and dangerous

Seamus Heaney[22]

In some ways this article can be read as counterpoint to Pamela Reynolds' work where she argues against the "cynicism that cancels" the children's "contribution to social and political change; and to meanness in failing to acknowledge courage and effort" because it shows the possible participation of children in social violence and their careless cruelty. Nonetheless, it is a counterpoint that her scholarship has enabled because it argues against the "passivity and innocence assigned to" children.[23]

Let me give a few additional examples to demonstrate the import of her theoretical and conceptual formulations. In November 2013, news of a successful sting operation on paedophiles broke across the media channels. The sting operation consisted of luring men into making sexual offers and comments online, sending sexually explicit pictures or asking the child to perform sexual acts for money over webcam. The operation was conducted via the internet, which allowed the addresses of the men's computers to be logged, their internet activities followed, and led to their eventual arrest. The child who posed as bait was not real but a computer generated image christened "Sweetie" whose responses were controlled by the organization who had masterminded the whole operation with the help of the police in several countries. A Dutch charity called Terre Des Hommes created Sweetie to look like a 10 year old Filipino girl through whom they would then make contact with men whose social network profiles had been watched and studied by the organization because they were suspected of perpetrating Child Sexual Abuse. More than a thousand men made contact with Sweetie and several arrests were made across the world, from Britain to Australia. Apart from the spectacular Orwellian orchestration of technology and policing, the complete erasure of actual children in this affair, let alone their agency and desire, to render desire prosecutable in the absence of actual harm done raises particular questions. This event underscores Pamela Reynolds' point that by attenuating the voice of the child, the state does not so much offer them protection, rather amplifies its disciplinary regimes to define norms, justify interventions, and link children to a normative project of social transformation.[24]

The second example I want to offer emerges from the context of a different scene of violence—the war on terrorism in Afghanistan. The thinly documented practice of *bacha bazi* in Afghanistan has found itself inadvertently attached to the global assemblage of the military-industrial complex that is fighting terrorism. Bacha bazi is alternately described as pederasty, dance performance, or Child Sexual Abuse and has resulted in a debate as to how the war in Afghanistan should address this practice or crime. Anthropological knowledge is necessary to describe this unstudied practice in a more nuanced way to prevent it from being pressed into service for war, racism, or even cultural relativism.[25] I mention these two instances of global policing and surveillance not to make any point apart from laying emphasis on the need for careful research on children and their sexual trajectories. Judgments that rest on notions of abuse of children based on universal pictures of innocence can be mobilized to have far-reaching repercussions.

Finally, no study of Pamela Reynolds' work would be complete without citing her discerning eye and use of an impressive range of poetry. I, too, find myself in a position to rely on one of her favourite poets to acknowledge the conceptual terrain she has charted and to say that the insights of her research are indeed an armourer's music that has set the craft of anthropology ringing.

Notes

[1] I wish to thank Zehra Nabi, Sahar Romani, Aditi Saraf, Megha Sehdev, and Gregory Sesek for their comments, edits, and encouragement on the earlier drafts of this paper.

[2] Gayatri Reddy, *With Respect to Sex: Negotiating Hijra Identity in South India* (Chicago: University of Chicago Press, 2005); Serena Nanda, *Neither Man nor Woman: The Hijras of India*, 2nd ed. (Belmont, CA: Wadsworth Pub. Co., 1999).

[3] James R. Kincaid, *Child-Loving: The Erotic Child and Victorian Culture* (Routledge, 1992); Joseph J. Fischel, *Sex and Harm in the Age of Consent* (Minneapolis: University of Minnesota Press, 2016).

[4] Lee Edelman, *No Future: Queer Theory and the Death Drive* (Durham: Duke University Press, 2004).

[5] Pamela Reynolds, "Children in Zimbabwe: Rights and Power in Relation to Work," *Anthropology Today* 1 (1985): 16-20.

[6] Pamela Reynolds, *Dance, Civet Cat: Child Labour in the Zambezi Valley* (London: Zed Books, 1991); Pamela Reynolds, "Learning to Listen," *Seminar* 546 (February 2005).

[7] Pamela Reynolds, "The ground of all making: state violence, the family and political activists," in *Violence and Subjectivity*, Veena Das, Arthur Kleinman, Mamphela Ramphele and Pamela Reynolds, eds. (Berkeley: University of California Press, 2000), 141-170, 157.

[8] Lawrence Cohen, "Love and the Little Line," *Cultural Anthropology* 26 (2011): 692-6; Lawrence Cohen, "Lucknow Noir," in *Homophobias: Lust and Loathing Across Time and Space*, David A. B. Murray, ed. (Durham:

Duke University Press, 2009); Lawrence Cohen, "Song for Pushkin," *Daedalus* 136 (Spring 2007): 103-15.

[9] Vaibhav Saria, "The Pregnant Hijra: Laughter, Dead Babies, and Invaluable Love," in *Living and Dying in the Contemporary World: A Compendium*, Veena Das and Clara Han, eds. (Berkeley: University of California Press, 2015).

[10] The figure of the mad old woman who was deemed to have psychiatric problems is ubiquitous in India and emblematic of the bad family that abandons their aged kin. Please see *No Aging in India: Alzheimer's, The Bad Family, and Other Modern Things* by Lawrence Cohen (1998) for a sharp analysis of gender, aging, and abandonment.

[11] I want to be careful how I frame this act of planned sexual violence. Legally, any sexual encounter with the mentally ill (but female) is considered rape since one party doesn't have the ability to consent and whenever the mentally ill elderly woman was raped, the people in the district headquarters used the word "rape". But I am not sure whether the young men who were joking about having sex with her even framed it in terms of committing violence. This was different from the way they would joke about raping the young girls and women of the village, those conversations would eroticize the violence and the lack of consent, as it would shore up their idea of romance and masculinity. I make this distinction to point out how the young men wrongly thought of sexual violence, rape, and consent. Till they had been caught and reprimanded, they did not see their plans as something violent, but at most a cruel joke, trick, or adventure. The incapacity of the elderly woman to consent made the planned act of sexual violence something other than their idea of rape as romance, or rape as revenge, or rape as formidable masculinity. They did not think of their planned escapade as rape even if others did, and consequently had to be taught so.

[12] Pratiksha Baxi, *Public Secrets of Law: Rape Trials in India* (Oxford University Press: New Delhi, 2014); Veena Das, "Sexual Violence,

Discursive Formations and the State," *Economic and Political Weekly* (1996) 2411-23.

[13] Ross Parsons, *Growing up with HIV in Zimbabwe: One Day This Will All Be Over* (Tamesis Books, 2012).

[14] Pamela Reynolds, "Activism, Politics and the Punishment of Children," in *Childhood Abused: Protecting Children against Torture, Cruel, Inhuman, and Degrading Treatment and Punishment*, Geraldine Van Bueren, ed. (Brookfield, VT: Ashgate, 1998).

[15] Pamela Reynolds, "Mapping the Conflict," in *anthropologies*, Todd Meyers and Richard Baxstrom, eds. (Baltimore, Maryland: Creative Capitalism, 2008), 57-79, 64.

[16] Baxi, *Public Secrets of Law*.

[17] The infamous 2012 Delhi gang rape also known as the Nirbhaya case is just one example where one of the perpetrators was below 18. My ethnographic incident of the young men deciding to rape the elderly woman at the train station was to flesh out the dangers resulting from ignoring the gender of the child at emphasizing age.

[18] Veena Das and Pamela Reynolds, "The Child on the wing: Children Negotiating the Everyday Geography of Violence." Background paper for research programme *Child on the Wing*, Department of Anthropology, Johns Hopkins University, 2003.

[19] Aaron Goodfellow, *Gay Fathers, their Children, and the Making of Kinship* (New York: Fordham University Press, 2015), 127.

[20] Pamela Reynolds, "Not known because not looked for': Ethnographers Listening to the Young in Southern Africa." *Ethnos* 60 (1995): 193-221.

[21] Pamela Reynolds, *Traditional Healers and Childhood in Zimbabwe* (Athens, OH: Ohio University Press, 1996).

[22] Seamus Heaney, *Field Work: Poems* (Macmillan, 2014).

[23] Pamela Reynolds, "Imfobe: Self-Knowledge and the Reach for Ethics among Former, Young Anti-Apartheid Activists," *Anthropology Southern Africa* 28 (2005): 62-72.

[24] Reynolds, "Imfobe."

[25] Samuel V. Jones, "Ending Bacha Bazi: Boy Sex Slavery and the Responsibility to Protect Doctrine," *Indiana International & Comparative Law Review* 25 (2015): 63-78; Samuel V. Jones, 2013. Men and Boys and the Ethical Demand for Social Justice. *Washington & Lee Journal of Civil Rights & Social Justice.* 20 (2013): 507; Sara L. Carlson, "To Forgive and Forget: How Reconciliation and Amnesty Legislation in Afghanistan Forgives War Criminals While Forgetting Their Victims," *Penn State Journal of Law & International Affairs.*1 (2012): xix.

5

An Anthropology of the Forms that Speak
Justice, Knowledge, Technique

Stefanos Geroulanos

I

I have to begin by explaining myself. I wrote my doctoral dissertation on antihumanism—the intellectual current that, as electrical ones do, first shocked established French thinkers when it coursed among the young in the 1920s and 1930s; and, then as they also do once the switch has not been toggled back to "off," seemed an established and unmovable light of its own. There came a moment during my dissertation-writing when I had become quite convinced by the merits of the argument, particularly the deep mistrust of established offers and programs of redemption, and it was then that I met Pamela Reynolds (met in the sense of more than a simple hello). I never studied with her properly; I studied after her. I read *Childhood in Crossroads* and *Dance Civet Cat* with two questions in mind: the first, how to think of the way that a study of people relates to a study of systems of thought, or even to mirror concepts back onto people; and the second, a question that Pamela posed over lunch one day, as I imagined aloud what I would do next and took down her notes. I will return to that question shortly.

She was completing the *War in Worcester*, which it's hard not to regard as a majestic work—this majesty is what I want to talk about here. Several years later, reading a draft introduction of that book, I was surprised to notice Pamela quote a specific passage, and comment: "There is, Emmanuel Levinas says, no 'transparency possible in method.' I take from this the suggestion that an approach to ethnographic fieldwork cannot be made completely explicit or justified as to why certain ways of proceeding were chosen."[1] By that time I was writing about transparency—about the ways in which French thinkers after World War II dismissed it, while others elsewhere in the Western world, and even the Soviet bloc, celebrated it. Transparency they held was impossible in one's approach, illusory in ethics, and destructive in politics: this was not a matter of transparent government, that German and American ideal that reigned supreme over much of the past decade, but of the imposition of a transparent, totalitarian society.

Beneath the crossfire of the political and moral priorities of *War in Worcester*—I still knew rather little of its details at the time, and more about the priorities—there lurked the question that Pamela Reynolds had asked me when I first mentioned my interest in transparency: *What about justice?* I wonder if she meant less to admonish me for my proclivity toward impossible, often unpolitical concepts, than that we usually think of justice requiring some—even *just a moment of*—transparency. At any rate, I find that question very difficult to answer, certainly in my work in conceptual history and the history of knowledge: concepts tend to vary in their consistency—sometimes they seem to dominate a particular discourse, sometimes they lose that thickness, become ghostly, refuse to be pinpointed. Some are local enough, others demand comparative work, and justice is one of those that bounce between the others and elide determination. I think Pamela found it difficult too in *War in Worcester*, for she pursued the problem by writing very clearly *around* it. Not in

96

the quotidian sense that it is easier to dodge justice and speak of injustice; rather, she translates it into a group of concepts: *struggle* and *injustice* and *pain*, and later in the book *imfobe* (grace) and *betrayal*. Not simply struggle against injustice, but both *struggle* as such, *injustice* as such, and so on; and yet the group only works as one, and only as guided toward the question of what justice might be, and a just approach, and a knowledge that does not forget that. One senses her characteristic gentle ferocity in articulating it, in intimately working-with her subjects, in asking them to remember pain. The struggle—the partisanship in it—here becomes something different than a presentation of oneself. Meanwhile, the very word "justice" almost never appears as such in the book. Only in titles of institutions, or quoted in appeals and official terms, is "justice" invoked—as well as in the negative.

II

Jacques Derrida apostrophizes the problem of justice, playing on the j in *justice* and in the first person singular *je*.

> Responsibility always seems to return to someone who says "I." This is how what is called law and perhaps justice work. This is how one understands the words of law, right, and justice in the culture where our tradition and language draw their breath.[2]

If I might put this in more abrasive terms, justice is too easily pasted onto a political commitment, a trust in my well-ordered society; too assured of its attachment to the right cause, and always committed at the same time to the difficulties all too evident in reality. What follows is a peculiar usurpation of responsibility: a scholar operates this in her epistemology in a manner that localizes often in advance the politics of identification. In politically tense subjects, this attachment of justice to one's politics is often explicit (or else we talk of a scholar's judiciousness) and yet if the political assemblage is worth anything, it is for that reason vulnerable. Indeed even if there can be no transparency in method, it is unduly difficult to think in a scholarly manner about justice.

Far be it for me to select a philosopher's approach and pursue their theory; Derrida's phrase has its virtue in its economy, but his way of retaining himself at once within and without seems to me very different from Pamela's. Besides distributing and questioning justice, she speaks both as herself and in collaboration with others, guiding them but also conveying them in this book. It is rather my point that we commit and claim justice as a matter of course; this becomes a trap in our technique. Similarly, a Rawlsian approach to distributive justice would fall into its own dragnet—in *War in Worcester*, every one of the hermeneutic successes of a Rawlsian position would endanger precisely the access force that Pamela manages to draw from her subjects and allies. If anything, fairness and distributive justice could be identified with the Truth and Reconciliation Commission's purposes, and hence with its myopia toward children's agency—so essential as much to the understanding of struggle and pain as to one of justice. Here is a passage that lets us see well through Pamela's crosshairs:

> Under apartheid, the people of Zwelethemba were fully aware of the injustice and immorality of the systems of control imposed on them. In their charges of injustice there is the sense of a failed accountability to those pressing the charge. A

sense, too, that society or something equivalent owes them an account of why these things happen.[3]

An account of why things happen; therefore, along with it, a technique to pursue and pattern that account. The thinkers and poets she cites, from Nyezwa to Adorno, Coetzee to Foucault, morph here into subjects and witnesses in their own turn, as though their speech hovered in ghostly fashion in the back of the room, speaking like the 14 young men that collaborated with her in reconstructing, in making this struggle and injustice and pain into knowledge. Justice as technique here becomes, in a paradoxical, skewed fashion, the basis for all knowledge, also what she elsewhere calls the ground of all making.

III

Could we speak of conceptual history in terms of the anthropology of conceptual persons? Of concepts as what fills the air in the room, what positions us in certain places in it rather than others? As what makes up the garments that clothe all speech, the sinews that end and tie together these garments and the cloth that makes them up?

In recent years, the prominence of the historian Reinhart Koselleck has renewed attempts to think the structuring and movement of concepts in European modernity. Koselleck focused, especially in his earlier career, on what he considered the concurrent stabilization and acceleration of temporal regimes in modernity, and recovered through concepts the basis of that movement.

The central concepts are improvement, development, progress, history itself, reform, crisis, evolution, and even revolution. Now it is precisely these concepts that, purely semantically, exercise a particularly stabilizing effect. They produce a certain linguistic unity in all political camps, even while there is argument about particulars.[4]

There is so much to praise in this approach, and several scholars have written in Koselleck's wake in a manner that is difficult to match. But in this classic passage the movement of concepts and meanings seems decided upon in advance. In that system all of the principal conceptual players come onto the stage at preordained metahistorical moments; concepts are neither agile nor local enough. They consistently elide more complex forms, the ways in which concepts yield to one another, remain attached to one another, thread across one another whole systems of thought or parts thereof. The elusiveness of concepts' historical shifts, appeal, and capacity for violence or disruption remains unstudied. We might look at concepts differently—in the way they play and mirror one another.

Imagine yourself in a house of mirrors, not unlike that in the climactic scenes of *The Lady from Shanghai* or in Bruce Lee's *Enter the Dragon*. The objects you see reflected in the mirrors don't easily appear on their own. Perhaps they are only reflected, over and over, each slightly differently reflected each time, differently distorted, next to other reflections of the same object, and often with different objects reflected alongside it. Reaching the object itself is often a difficult exercise, despite its multiple appearances. Its imagos are just as valuable as the object itself; and so are the images surrounding its own image on the surface of each mirror. Intentions, playful or murderous hide between the mirrors. In the house of mirrors each of us sees ourselves reflected as well, not least as we orient ourselves vis-à-vis these mirrors themselves and the reflections. Together, the mirrors stage our intrusion, that is, our presence as it reorients the universe of reflections. And then there are the tains, cracks, nicks in the mirrors: the scene as I see it reflected is always modified, always reduced; and conversely, the object itself is formed through these reductions in which I, the interpreter, participate.

Why play on this point, why prioritize this image? This mirroring effect—the ever-receding, illusory, reflective universe that concepts establish and in particular the capacity of certain concepts to live inside others, inside other figures and formulations, to be mediated by others, not merely tied to these others but hidden in them, refracted through them, mutated by them, even gorgonized by them. Studying concepts means becoming involved in this play of mirrors; as other concepts change, so does the concept shift when we are looking for it because of its reflections, the concepts to which it relates.

IV

If this all sounds abstract or figurative, I promise it's not simply theoretical: it is to me analogous to what Pamela writes when she notes, while observing the Truth and Reconciliation Commission:

> An ethnographic study of the Commission constituted a strange piece of fieldwork. Being a detached observer of the TRC hearings was distressing. I knew but a few of the testifiers and made no attempt to meet others, not wishing to intrude during anguished times. The hearings filled me with ambivalence about the Commissioners' roles and my own. I

was particularly troubled by the realization that the testimonies were like snippets from a collage, cut out of time, place, history, relationships, contingency, choice, and pattern. The general subsumed the particular.[5]

That is the experience, I like to think, of work within concepts; it is an experience of responsibility, of its assignation and distribution, and also of functioning without a given ground—a situation where the off-kilter position of the anthropologist at once urges closer attention, from different angles, and destabilizes the promise, redemption, and even narrative on offer. The entire point of a concept history would be an anthropology of the forms that speak—even to make them speak without losing track of how the one who speaks is wrapped in them just as they are "wrapped in pain."[6] Pain does not apply to concepts as it does to bodies; but it does not follow that they don't partake of it, just as they partake of a problem such as that of justice. And it is here that the elusiveness of concepts, their capacity to leave us thinking we'd answered the broad question, effected the "stabilizing effect," while they change sides and buttress better a different narrative: such are the tricksters that perhaps over- and under-determine violence, and perhaps healing too. The mirrors involved in an operation such as that of the TRC, with the well-meaning (and culturally transformative) usurpation of these concepts of "truth" and "reconciliation," in their appeal for a "new" nation, also guide Pamela to ask how she might reconstruct and reappreciate the way they make meaning from a perspective where meaning is not managed, and where the promised narrative and chance at redemption do not hold. These concepts in conflict—mirrored, embattled, violent, promising then appear

102

at every turn: and justice in this case resides behind truth and reconciliation in a sense inapplicable to the TRC and its overarching narrative. As I also wrote early in this essay, it is not that Pamela identifies injustice and avoids justice: rather she pursues it doggedly but with an awareness of its capacity to escape her once captured: *imfobe* and betrayal join the pressure of struggle and the new faces of injustice. When a different narrative needs to be reconstructed, pursued behind the sentinels of official speech, when it needs to be offered for the possibility of some reclamation and some living-together, concepts are hijacked, and reconstructed from below. So, indeed there ought not to be justice for concepts; as "clothes" they are armor and weaponry, offensive but also counteroffensive. Yet there is at times justice through them, awaiting a fictional selfhood in awaiting to become narratives to justify, figures to make selfhood in the face of sovereign and structural violence.

It is possible that "living beside" (despite betrayal) tells us something other than or more than the lack of revenge. Perhaps in this context of multiple structures of loyalty, obedience, and respect, there were disjunctions, conjunctions, and coincidences that stretched its meanings. Some structures (the apartheid state) were fought, and others (kinship, filial, and communal loyalty) glued or shredded responses. Despite the fact that many kinds of trust could be and were betrayed, a certain clarity in resistance held. In the tumult and chaos of conflict, state oppression, and social disorder, selves were constructed and reconstructed. The fashioning of identity and the reorganization of social forms, albeit embattled and weakened, occurred in the face of repression and terror, and morals were reworked, examined, and deployed even as attempts were made, or so it seemed, to bring about social dissolution.[7]

The narrative end, and practice, of "living beside" bridges these different forms. In it, struggle and pain and injustice are felt (and pursued) by actual persons, and a story of trust, proximity and life amidst betrayal holds together against social dissolution. What the historian of concepts cannot offer, Pamela does with grace: reconstruct the form in which actual and present extensions of this struggle continue not only in scholarship, but in a participatory reformulation of these selves that gives the possibility of a tomorrow.

Notes

[1] Pamela Reynolds, *War in Worcester: Youth and the Apartheid State* (New York: Fordham University Press, 2013), 3.

[2] Jacques Derrida, "Justices" in *Critical Inquiry* 31 (Spring 2005), 289.

[3] Reynolds, *War in Worcester*, 109.

[4] Reinhart Koselleck, "Linguistic Change and the History of Events" published in *The Journal of Modern History* (Dec., 1989).

[5] Reynolds, *War in Worcester*, 162.

[6] Fiona Ross and Pamela Reynolds, "Wrapped in pain: Moral Economies and the South African TRC," in *Context* 3 (1991): 1-9.

[7] Reynolds, *War in Worcester*, 132.

6

The Anthropologist Fashions and Refashions, is Fashioned and Refashioned

Todd Meyers talks with Pamela Reynolds

Students in Elizabeth Goodenough's course on Childhood and Conflict at the University of Michigan organized and recorded the interview between Professors Meyers and Reynolds in October 2015. The focus of the interview is on Professor Reynolds' book, *War in Worcester* (Fordham University Press, 2012; University of KwaZulu-Natal Press, 2014). The book combines a study of the Truth and Reconciliation Commission's (TRC) findings on the stand taken by South African youth with extended fieldwork conducted with fourteen young men who were involved in the struggle in a small town in the Western Cape. Under Apartheid, the South African government gave no quarter to the young fighters. Indeed, it targeted them. Security Forces meted out cruel treatment to those who rebelled, incarcerated even the very young under dreadful conditions, and used torture frequently. *War in Worcester* problematises the use of the term "victim" for the political engagement of young people and encourages fresh analysis of the kind of revolt being enacted elsewhere in the world, such as North Africa and the Middle East.

The following conversation has been edited for clarity.

Todd Meyers [TM]:
Pamela, thank you very much for the opportunity to talk

with you. I am going to ask you a number of questions, many of which are taken or paraphrased from students in Elizabeth Goodenough's "Children in Conflict" seminar—but first, maybe one way into your work on the anthropology of childhood, on young men and women, is your own childhood growing up in Rhodesia. I'm curious about the things that shaped you intellectually, the things that may have shaped you as an anthropologist.

Pamela Reynolds [PR]:
Well, I'm one of the last of the children of the colonial empire. I was born in Rhodesia a long time ago and I had parents who were not left-leaning in any sense, went along with the colonial project within Rhodesia. I guess the first memory I have of objecting to all of that was when I was four. I was sitting in the garden with my nanny and we both decided to have a pee, although I knew my father would be furious if he saw us, and I said to her, "Do you have any children?" She said, "Yes I do" and I said, "Where are they," and she said, "With my mother in the countryside." I was shocked, here she was looking after me and her children were in the countryside.

By the age of thirteen I knew that I could never have another discussion on politics with my parents. I think that I formed different views through reading. I was a shy child and no doubt I hid myself in books. Neither of my parents had had the opportunities I enjoyed.

TM: During your seminar earlier this week, one of the students asked about how the young men that you worked with in the project that would become *War in Worcester* read you politically, how they scrutinized your political leanings and perspectives. Did your own childhood, one that was in its own way set against this colonial project, even as a very young person, bring you closer to these men? —Was there common ground? And how did they understand your history in relationship to their respective experiences or was that something that was ever discussed?

PR: I don't really know how the men read me politically. Towards the end of the first intensive years together they called me a radical. I was not clear quite what they meant but they said I would always be in trouble with institutions. I guess they were right in that I went my own way and spoke out against what I thought was wrong. Spoke from the edge, maybe. They certainly scrutinized my political understanding especially during group meetings. Perhaps as a child my arrival at political positions askew with those in power leant me an understanding that the men could acknowledge. They may have understood my history in relation to the projects I had already undertaken, particularly the study of children in Crossroads when, in defiance of the state, people were establishing an unauthorised settlement; and the research I did with young people who emerged from prisons, some after many years of incarceration in consequence of their activism, and immediately became students at the University of Cape Town. I had also worked with indigenous healers who were engaged in community healing in the aftermath of the war of liberation in Zimbabwe. In my experience conducting research in southern Africa I have found that if my interest in a specific topic is judged to be deep enough then people will initially accept me and trust will emerge as we work on the project and they grant that it is their project. Obviously, I've depended on their trust of me for my very safety.

TM: Trust is such a major part of *War in Worchester*. Trust casts very long shadows, through betrayals, across relationships that evolve and dissolve. I'm probably putting the cart before the horse, but could you talk a little about the project itself? I'm curious about how it began and the questions that you had going in, as well as what questions grew from the years you worked with these men?

PR:I was fascinated by the fact that the young had the strength to take on the state and to sustain their rebellion; that they had the confidence to deliberately cause trouble and face, unarmed, the Security Forces; and that they had the ability to stand together down time. When the Truth and Reconciliation Commission (TRC) was formed I decided to work alongside it and find out in detail how the youth had fought against the apartheid state. My initial interest focused on how the young built and maintained sufficient force to withstand the government's retaliation; how they established connections, co-operation, a sense of belonging and continuity; how they attracted support, selected leaders, formulated rules of engagement and responses to the tactics of the opposition; how they set up networks of information and contact; and how they dealt with the resistance of their parents and the older generation put forward largely in fear for their lives. Later I became interested in issues of time, danger, self-recrimination and reactions to betrayal as well as the lack of government support for youth in the aftermath. It was a two-pronged study; one was of the Commission and one of a group of young men undertaken because I grew disappointed in the Commission and what it was achieving in terms of finding out about youth. I worked in a small township called Zwelethemba on the edge of a town,

Worcester, in the hinterland of Cape Town and the question I was asking was for them to tell their stories about how they operated and it was fascinating work. The conflict had ended only six years prior to our study. One knows from the aftermath of the holocaust how long it took for many people to begin to talk about their experiences and yet here was the TRC (and I) asking people to tell us about traumatic experiences. I sought, in particular, to find out how fourteen young men fought in the 1980s in the context of the community in which they lived.

TM: I know that you left disappointed and very critical of the TRC, but surely this is not how you went in. Did your criticisms grow over time? What things were particularly discouraging?

PR: I hoped that I could discover from the Truth and Reconciliation Commission's investigation how the young had conducted their mass stand over time and against terrible reprisals. I began by following the TRC Hearings on Human Rights Violations that had been committed under apartheid. I became a peripatetic groupie. It seemed to me that the nature and design of the Hearings did not allow for the gathering of the data in the way that met my interests. I became critical and sometimes my criticisms were heeded by the Commissioners. I think one can be critical of any such commission. It is an enormously difficult exercise to conduct and I have great admiration for what the Commissioners and the staff achieved in accumulating a vast amount of knowledge about what had happened in the immediate past right back to 1960. My criticism revolved around the manner in which they treated the youth or failed to treat the youth and therefore that's when I decided to parallel the study of the TRC with a much more intensive study of young activists in the small suburb ("township") of Zwelethemba.

TM: One of the objectives of the Commission was to document but the work you did with these fourteen young men was surely a different kind of archive or record. But I'm curious how you imagined this different kind of documenting?

PR: I think that, perhaps, the biggest mistake that the architects of the Act that established the Truth and Reconciliation Commission made was to take from the United Nations and International Law the categorisation of people involved in armed conflict as either civilian or soldier and they termed it, in South Africa, as victim and perpetrator. The youth were placed under the category of victim and many of them rejected it and refused to give evidence before the Commission. I worked with people categorised as victims which was not one that they applied to themselves; they saw themselves as warriors against the state. And once the category of victim is established then the focus falls on incidents of violence. The problem there is that the instances were frequently examined out of context, at least out of the context of political activism. The men in Zwelethemba said, "We were the legitimate enemy of the state." Some of them agreed to testify at the Hearing held in Worcester and some refused saying that it was not an establishment before which they were prepared to speak. A variety of methods for gathering data was used particularly by the Commission's Research wing. The TRC used oral evidence from ten percent of the respondents; the evidence was heard in public and it received a wide distribution in the country. The TRC reached a broad swathe of people through public attendance at the Hearings which were held across the country in a variety of venues; they were recorded live on radio and gathered a strong following; there was a weekly television programme that showed videos shot during the Hearings; public debates were organised and publications put out. In contrast, I, apart from following the Commission, undertook research in a small area with a small sample of fourteen men who had been recognised in their community during the conflict as local leaders. The activists and I set out to examine the recent past over time. I worked closely with each of them and with a few at a time and with all of them together to establish individual and group relationships. We discussed their entry into activism and their experiences across stretches of ten to fifteen years of engagement. I created specific tools to capture aspects of the struggle, for example, the use of municipal maps to trace their battles and the recording of time-lines. We filled in TRC forms together at their request and I surveyed the context in ways that anthropologists do.

TM: One of the things I find so fascinating about the book is that you show the kind of labour in which these young men are engaged, not just to occupy this different role of fighter vs. victim, but also to inhabit that role in various contexts across the relationships of those fourteen men, across the small generational gradations between them: the older boys and the younger boys sort of grew a different kind of history together, through the histories that they're telling and working so hard against, pushing against those generalisations what it means to be a victim and what it means to be a fighter. In some ways this extends a question that Sophia, one of the students in the class, asked, "How did each man suffer and heal differently?" Part of this project, which I think so critical and crucial, is the way in which you show that the men fashioned themselves through their different relationships to the conflict, and through their different relationships to one another, so that suffering and healing are shown in the fine grain of relationships, which are at times very different from one another, rather than creating general categories of suffering and healing that contain everything and say nothing.

PR: You have answered Sophia's question well. There was a marked difference in the ways the men handled suffering and its effects as well as in the process of healing. Perhaps our joint sessions offered a safe place to talk about the past and share experiences. What is most interesting about the project is that the fourteen men and I would meet often. Frequently I would make an appointment with one of them and all of them would turn up. What I had anticipated to be an interview with one man became, instead, a group session. One would have thought it foolish to design so many group sessions especially that began at an early stage in the research and especially, when one was dealing with torture, pain and betrayal. The men would gather and they would often interrogate me before they began to talk. And the interrogation would go on for some time as to who I was and why I was there and what the world was saying about the Truth Commission and what therapy really meant. And then after a while the more senior would take the session in hand and with acuity and tact they would bring everybody back to the topic at hand but never entirely my topic - they wouldn't answer questions about chronology or kinship or any of these things that anthropologists look at but they would talk about the past and the manner in which they fought and the relationships they established and the fact that they had held through those years together. As you say, they represented a wide variety of persons but there was a level of acceptance among them that was extraordinary and, indeed, one of them had betrayed another one within the group, I was told, but neither the one betrayed nor betrayer said anything to me about it yet they worked together; that was amazing in itself. I think, with time, with the Commission explicitly providing a platform on which stories about violations could be told, people began to open up about the cruelty they had experienced. It had been the ethos of the Liberation Organisations not to talk about one's pain, to be silent about it, because one had not suffered as much as the person in the next cell and one must not propagate the manner in which the state was causing terror. And there is, too, a notion within some societies in southern Africa called *hlonipha* that has to do with categories of people, according to age, status, gender and so on, who may or may not talk to each other. It could, for example, have been tricky for the young men to talk about intimate matters before me, an older, white woman. Slowly constraints fell away and the men began to talk about the actual pain and humiliation. Gradually the differences among them emerged and various levels of leadership were identified and the character of each man's cognisance of and articulation about politics and ethics. Given the format and scope of the Commission, it was unable to take into account changes over time. I should like to note that we shared a formal intimacy as befit our differences in age, gender and experience.

TM: This is key. It is one thing to critique a kind of bureaucratic technology of a survey or a form you know is already limited—they always are. But it's this element of time that seems so crucial, and also the work of memory, that is so easily lost. One of the things that your book does very subtly is to move in time with these men. As you are collectively moving forward in time, they're also reaching back into their own memories, to the time in which they were quite young, but they're also moving forward in time, so it's a work not just of their relationship to the apartheid state, in real time that evolves as you followed them, but also in that time of memory as it evolves and gets refashioned and in some ways overwritten during the time that you know them. When you bring up the issue of trust it's not simply the trust of an anthropologist gaining the trust of these young men, but it's trust in a way in which they begin to occupy a new domain of telling that blends both the political discourse in which they were so invested and the revelations about their own experiences of betrayal under torture, the messiness and vulnerability of real trust, which is not so different from the trust the TRC asked of people when they would document their stories, to very different ends. Would you talk a little about your sensibility as an anthropologist? How do you approach these things? I know you don't think about these relationships simply in terms of research subject and researcher. There's intimacy, not just personal intimacy, but an intimacy with questions and concepts.

PR: Your observations are insightful – that the men began "to occupy a new way of telling" and that there was "an intimacy with questions and concepts". What does it mean to be intimate with these? It implies a knowing, a kinship –

perhaps a claustrophobic one as with a torturer who is also a kinsman, to be close to, to be experienced in.... The sort of questions and concepts that come to mind include morality, trust, oppression, rejection, adrenalin or the self-consciousness that accompanies fear, instinct, loyalty. Their experience was different from mine and all that I could offer was a setting in which to consider such intimacies and to do so, as it turned out, in the company of those with similar patterns of experience. I think the essence of all of that is a relationship between me and each man and then of course among themselves building afresh on an existing relationship. The relationship entails questioning and the danger, of course, is intrusion and bias and, you know, who am I to ask those questions and why should they answer them and why should they tell the truth as they see it? I think that time allowed us to trail across those issues and arrive at various positions; various points that reflect one on another and eventually allow one to actually know where to step in and what to ask. It's a matter of learning what questions to ask. I think that is what anthropology is about. Philosophers claim they do it, too. Relationships are the hub in this project. I am told that I demand a lot from relationships. The demand is to know as accurately as possible; the challenge is to make a fair demand in relation to what one needs to know. Is it one that the other accepts? Is there, as Lévinas would ask, responsibility for the other between the two of us? I think that's the essence of what one has to do in undertaking a project like this of such delicacy and with a strong possibility of stirring pain unnecessarily. I set out with the intention of not asking about pain partly because I had done another study with people who had been tortured and I thought I knew enough about it, thank you, from an earlier study of activists emerging in the early 1990s from prison. But pain came up all the time, how could it not? In contrast to gradually being able to come to know each other over time, I was asked to help people in the community of Zwelethemba to fill in the second round of forms that the Truth Commission sent out for people who had been declared "victims" to complete. The task meant that I worked with people I did not know and it was extremely difficult because we hadn't built trust. I would sit there and read out the questions on the forms and ask for response even to questions that I found deeply distressing. The forms were very ill devised it seemed to me. Initially the TRC had promised to ask for accounts of violence only once in the presence of trained therapists. I remember sitting in a room with a woman whose son had been shot in the community, just shot on the streets, and the question was, "Do you still feel pain about the loss of your son?" and she just let out a terrible high-pitched scream – how could she not? She and I sat with tears running down our cheeks as her young kinsman handed us tissues. It was the only time in all those years that I cried.

TM: Did the fourteen men quiz you about your past?

PR: Absolutely, they quizzed me about everything. Yeah they did, but never really accusing me of being the wrong sort of person to be there. I, the older, white woman asking about their past—it was never an issue.

TM: Wow. I want to ask you another question from the students. What did the young men think of all of this in the end? You produced this wonderful ethnography, and I know that they were in conversation with you over time about its development, but what did they think about all of this in the end?

PR: When the manuscript of the book was ready, we met again and I talked about it and gave each one a copy. After some time, we held another meeting and responses to the manuscript were aired. Only matters of fact were requested. Some of the men had died and family members read the manuscript and responded to it. The men told me that the process leading up to the writing of the book had been a gift in the sense that it had held them together in that community and they'd worked together. It was the early time of the spread of AIDS and they had worked together on educating people about it and they held discussions on other facets of community life, which would not have happened had they not been held together around a specific project. They were fourteen of the local leaders, the ones who still lived in the community after freedom had been secured.

TM: This is a slightly different question, but I am curious to know if they recognised you as an educator?

PR: Do you mean the people in the community?

TM: People in the community, these men. I guess I'm asking you more generally about your thoughts on being an educator?

PR: It was known that I was a professor at the University of Cape Town and that therefore I was seen to be a teacher and, I guess, an emissary from the outside. Two of the men were studying at the university; one did an Honours degree at which I taught; a third had studied for a while at the University of the Western Cape. I faced a knowing public. It was clear to the men what I was trying to do. I don't think that I educated them: we were in dialogue – the 15 of us and the relationships between us criss-crossed the terrain of our engagement. It is hard to say what the members of the community thought of me; I was never challenged or made to feel unwelcome. Oddly enough it was recently, a few years after the project was formally over that a drunk man came up to me after a meeting between the men and told me I was unwelcome in the area and I ought to leave. Xolile was saying goodbye to me and, in his gentle way, he put his arm around the man's shoulders saying, "She is our teacher and is here at our invitation". The man was mollified. I would introduce myself as anthropologist - nobody ever knows what it means, even we don't. The community accepted my presence because the men accepted me and they were respected by most people. There were few occasions during my years of research when I met with resistance. The police and government officials caused me more trouble than anyone else. Once an official threatened to bulldoze my room in Crossroads, then an illegal squatter settlement, and the local council *toyi-toyied* on my behalf. Some irony there. Some of the places I worked were dangerous, actually. During the years under apartheid I did research in places in which I was forbidden to be. For example, in a brief study that I undertook in order to write a paper for The Second Carnegie Inquiry into Poverty and Development in South Africa in 1984, I decided to find out from men who lived in the housing that was built for them by the government or by companies in which they were denied the right to have their wives and children. Only someone from the "Homelands", the Bantustans, who had a job and housing was allowed to live in the cities. Their wives and their children were supposed to stay in those fictive Homelands. The men usually saw them for three weeks a year when on leave over the Christmas holidays. It was a draconian system. I wanted to capture their thoughts on being denied the right to have their children grow up alongside them. I resolved to go at night to the hostels (the men worked during the day) to talk to them. This was in the early 1980s. I was living, once more, in Zimbabwe and had experienced difficulty in obtaining a visa to enter South Africa. Entry for me into a township was disallowed and entry into hostels at night was to court trouble. An African man, a teacher, and I went into the hostels and we asked people to gather together to discuss one question: "What do you feel about being denied the right to be with your children?" A few of them would stand up and object and say, "Who are you? How could you come and ask us now? We're tired and we've got to find our supper?" "What are you doing here?" and other men would say, "No, no, no this is an important question, we're going to answer this question". And they talked very beautifully. One of them said, "We are men spilt like water in the sand." And every time I said something that seemed to steer away from the topic they'd haul me back in again. The focus was not at all on relationship, only on a single question. After about ten nights at the end of a session with seventy men, I was driving my companion home when the police stopped us, one police van in front and one at the back of the car. They demanded to know where we had been so I lied and said, "We have been to a church meeting and I am taking my colleague home." They yelled at him, "Get out the car and walk home" and he said he wouldn't, he didn't want to, he was objecting and I had to say to him quietly, "We have all of these notes and these tapes from seventy men at your feet. We can't possibly let the police get hold of them. I'm afraid we'll both have to do what they say." He climbed out of the car and he began to walk. I still feel deeply ashamed about having made him do that. Then the police questioned me. They said, "If you're ever caught in any township again you will be put straight into prison." I was back there the next night. In that scenario the people with whom I talked didn't know me and I simply took it on trust that they would respond. In my major studies I worked for long periods of time within communities and I was protected by them.

TM: I think this characterises your work, not only the intensity, but also the intimacy and the closeness. One of the things I know as your student, one of the things that many of us learned from you and your work, is a kind of a burden of proof. I'm thinking specifically about your work on child labour. Anyone can say, "this and this is the way in which a child works throughout the day" and "this is the labour of a child," but you give proof. When asked by critics to prove it, you've done so in the most obsessive and thorough way, which still scares students when they read some of your work, but that's also a kind of burden of proof in anthropology.

There are also other moments, I don't know if I would call them missteps, but moments when we stumble into the narrative of telling in your work, when the fullness of these stories reveals itself, a different proof, including accounting for difficulty and why difficultly emerges. You know it's one thing to talk about work and difficult circumstances, and quite another to talk about what those circumstances really mean and the kinds of relationships that are forged or frayed over time. I don't really have a question, it's more of a comment, but please disabuse me if I'm totally wrong.

PR: Yeah, well, my youngest daughter says that I was totally irresponsible. There's an interesting piece in Malinowski's diary about his purchases at a chemist in Australia before he left for the islands; he bought cocaine and, I don't know, about four kinds of drugs and a bunch of medicines. I went to the chemist in Harare and purchased plasters and aspirins and that's all despite the fact that I was setting off to live in the Zambezi Valley on the edge of a wild game reserve in an area in which endemic illnesses are rife. If anything had happened to me, it would have taken half a day to get to a hospital. My daughter was right though I am not sure whether Malinowski or I was the more irresponsible.

TM: You were quizzed by fourteen young men and four daughters, who I imagine quizzed you just as intensely about what you were up to.

PR: When my daughters crossly asked why I had arrived home from the field so late one night, I knew that old age had set in. In 1992, I think, no 1982 I began to work with indigenous healers in an area 80 kilometres east of Harare.

TM: What's a decade or two?

PR: In 1981 I returned with my family to live in Zimbabwe (I had left the country in 1967) and, the next year, I began to work as a lowly researcher at the University of Zimbabwe, just after the end of the war between the government and liberation forces. My research topic was on the treatment by healers of children and how they trained certain children in the arts of healing. The area where I worked had been carved out as a Tribal Trust Land by the colonial powers. It had been an especially active arena during the war and the local counsellors welcomed me but insisted that I take a room in the small town of Musami because it was too dangerous for me to live outside of the village, as I had wanted to do. A room that had been a servant's quarter behind a bar was selected for my occupation. As it was situated behind a bar, the noise often drove me out to walk in the evening to outlying homesteads thus defeating the intention of the kind counsellors. President Mugabe's long reign had recently begun and he was attempting to mould the two liberation forces, ZANU and ZAPU, into a single army by intermingling the followers in a number of camps one of which was quite near the village. One night the one group rebelled and shot over twenty members of the other group and then ran away. The next morning, I found camouflage boots and clothing scattered around the streams in the bush. So that night I went to my tiny room and I wondered if I should shut the window against the absconding soldiers but it was hot so I didn't. In the middle of the night, the door was flung open and I leapt up from the camp bed, took my best karate stance and looked towards the door only to see the beautiful eyes of a cow staring at me. She'd been rubbing her back on my door. That's how brave I was.

TM: I had the privilege of reading parts of the diary that you're preparing for publication from your time in the Zambezi Valley. Could you talk a little bit about the diary and the motivations for preparing it?

PR: My intention in writing the diary in 1984–1985 was to trace my thoughts while researching child labour among the Tonga people of Omay in the Nyaminyami District of the Zambezi Valley. In fact, it became a record of my observations of and responses to the daily happenings among members of the twelve families with whom I worked and the villagers of Chitenge. The motivation to publish it is twofold: one to record the precariousness of children's lives two generations after the homes and lands of the Valley Tonga were drowned under Lake Kariba; and the other motive is to record the life patterns and experiences of children in the Valley for the archive. The Tonga people had lived on the banks of the Zambezi River for over two thousand years. In the 1950s the World Bank, the British Government and the client Governments of Southern and Northern Rhodesia decided to create a huge lake to give hydroelectric power to Zambia (formerly Northern Rhodesia) and to Zimbabwe (formerly Southern Rhodesia). In doing so they dislocated over 56,000 Tonga people moving them away from the banks of the river. In Southern Rhodesia they were placed in the dry hinterland where soils were sandy, where the heat was intense, where the rainfall was low and unpredictable, where there was scant water and where they were no longer able to hunt or to fish at will or able to grow two crops a year on the flood plain of the Zambezi River. The Tonga are resourceful and strong and have created communities that, when the crops are good, hold up a viable way of life. Nevertheless, there is a level of poverty and a lack of access to proper infrastructure, including adequate medical care, education and basic amenities for all that is unacceptable especially given the vast resources stolen from them. The diary records this. I would write the diary at night sitting on the narrow balcony of my thatched house on stilts sipping a tot of whisky from a crystal glass as I watched the drama of African sunsets. The diary was supposed to help me plan my research and reflect on what to do next but, of course, it ended up with me whining about the crocodile tails and slimy ochre I had to eat and the minor annoyances of everyday life, like living in close proximity to two snakes for three months; and the magic of early morning walks into the valley behind my house among wild animals and birds; and the pleasure I had experienced; and the people with whom I had talked. In a way it's another record of a white woman "bravely living alone" in Africa. I thought of calling the diary *The Timid Anthropologist in Africa* because I was both timid and intrepid in a somewhat irresponsible way.

Afterword

Pamela Reynolds

The book is a contribution to the grand scheme that Francis Nyamnjoh outlined at the conference in Buea. The roll call he sets before anthropologists in Africa is daring, demanding and finely crafted. Here we address but one aspect of it – the theme of intergenerational conversations, particularly on the transmission of knowledge. He asks us to elaborate in discussing the process of transmission on what the lessons are for, why one writes and for whom. In doing so he raises the question of belonging ("Where one's umbilical cord was buried.") Tracing the origins of the five essayists illustrates the fertile muddle of origins: they were born in Zimbabwe, the USA, Swaziland and India of parents that hailed from numerous countries. The knowledge they have garnered and are now transmitting to yet another generation is based on research and intellectual interactions in Africa, China, India, France, Greece, Britain and the USA. Francis generously calls this volume a "testament to the infinite spectrum of possibilities available for disciplinary renewal".

I had the good fortune of learning from teachers at the University of Cape Town, Harvard and the Delhi School of Economics, particularly Monica Wilson, Erik Erickson, Paolo Freire, Veena Das, and from Africa's activists and writers, some of whom I knew. I learned as much from students and the people with whom I engaged in pursuing "the imprudent and wonderful labour" that Todd Meyers calls anthropology. "We have to hope," Ali Smith writes, "…that the people who love us a little bit will in the end have seen us truly. In the end not much else matters".[1] In the essays published here my work has been seen truly, indeed expanded upon, by those far younger than I. I am honoured.

Teaching is a privilege although an essayist in this book once said, "Your undergraduate course was fantastic. I was the only one who understood it." The privilege comes from borrowing the brilliance of young minds. Sylvain Perdigon called the graduate course I had led when I joined the faculty at Johns Hopkins University, "Enigmatic." He said, "You gave an intense talk for fifteen minutes then stopped." I knew that the group of graduates was extraordinary and that the seminars would contain scintillating dialogue and I was right. Todd was one of the group. Todd's wisdom, efficiency and generosity is attested to here.

Note

[1] Ali Smith, *Autumn* (New York: Pantheon, 2016), 160.

Pamela Reynolds

CV & Selected Bibliography

Curriculum Vitae

Narrative Biography

Pamela Reynolds is an Anthropologist who has worked in the field of the Ethnography of Childhood in southern Africa for decades. Her work has taken her to strange places and entangled her in fascinating situations that stirred both danger and laughter. Among children she found that the ordinary is often extraordinary.

Pamela has five degrees, she has written five books, she has taught at five universities and has four (not five) daughters.

Qualifications

University of Cape Town	History	Bachelor of Art, 1965
University College London	Education	Certificate of Education, 1966
University of Cape Town	Education	Bachelor of Education, 1968
Harvard University	Education	Master of Education, 1970
University of Delhi	Anthropology	Master of Literature, 1974
University of Cape Town	Anthropology	Doctor of Philosophy, 1984

Appointments

2002-2009: Professor, Johns Hopkins University, Department of Anthropology

2001-2002: Presidential Visiting Professor, International Institute, University of Michigan, Ann Arbor

2000-2001: Visiting Professor, Department of Anthropology, University of California, Berkeley

1998-2000: Professor and Head of Department, Department of Social Anthropology, University of Cape Town

1991-1997: Senior Lecturer and Associate Professor, Department of Social Anthropology, University of Cape Town

1994: Visiting Research Fellow, University of Amsterdam

1997: Guest Lecturer, University College London

1984-1991: Director of Childhood Action, Research and Documentation Institute

1987-1988: Director, Ford Foundation and South Africa Save-the-Children Project in Zambezi Valley

1984-1986: Senior Research Fellow, Faculty of Agriculture, University of Zimbabwe Research on Childhood, Labour and Social Change

1982-1983: Research Fellow, Faculty of Social Science, University of Zimbabwe

1975: Consultant on Education, Indian Institute of Management, Ahmedabad

Grants and Awards

2010: Honorary Professor in Anthropology, University of Cape Town.

2009: Emerita Professorship, Johns Hopkins University.

2008: Visiting Professor from June 2008 to January 2009 at the Children's Institute, University of Cape Town.

2001: Presidential Professorship at the University of Michigan, Ann Arbor, from September 2001 to June 2002 to lead a series of bi-weekly seminars on 'Contested Childhoods'. The Mellon Foundation supported the series with a generous grant.

1999: Fellowship Award from All Souls College, Oxford, January to July 1999.

1997: Harry F. Guggenheim Award for "An Ethnographic Study of the Truth and Reconciliation Commission".

1996: Anglo-American Chairman's Fund Award.

1996: Ernest Oppenheimer Memorial Trust Award.

1995: Centre for Science Development. Award for the Study of the Truth and Reconciliation Commission.

1995: Fellow of the University of Cape Town (awarded for life).

Selected Bibliography

Books

The Uncaring, Intricate World, with essays by Todd Meyers, Achille Mbembe, Julie Livingston, and Jane Guyer. Duke University Press, forthcoming.

War in Worcester. Youth and the Apartheid State. Fordham University Press, 2013 and KwaZulu-Natal Press, 2014.

Traditional Healers and Childhood in Zimbabwe. Ohio University Press, 1996.

Dance Civet Cat: Child Labour in the Zambezi Valley. London, Zed Press (with Ohio University Press and Baobab Publications), 1991.

Lwaano Lwanyika: The Tonga Book of the Earth (with Colleen Crawford Cousins). Harare, 1991. Two editions published: one in English and one in Tonga. Republished by the International African Institute and PANOS in 1993 for worldwide distribution.

Childhood in Crossroads: Cognition and Society in South Africa. Cape Town, David Philip (with W. B. Eerdmans), 1989.

Growing Up in a Divided Society: The Contexts of Childhood in South Africa (edited with Sandra Burman). Johannesburg, Ravan Press, 1986. Re-issued in hardback and paperback by Northwestern University Press (with a new Preface by Robert Coles), 1990.

Edited volumes

Remaking a World: Violence, Social Suffering and Recovery, edited with Veena Das, Arthur Kleinman, Margaret Lock, and Mamphela Ramphele. University of California Press, 2001.

Violence and Subjectivity, edited with Veena Das, Arthur Kleinman, Margaret Lock, Mamphele Ramphela. University of California Press, 2000.

Editorships

Guest Editor with Olga Nieuwenhuys and Karl Hanson. *Childhood*, Special Issue on "Childhood Rights in International Development," August 2006, Volume 13, Issue 3.

Guest Editor with Nancy Scheper-Hughes. "Reconstructing Communities in Crisis." *Human Rights Journal*, Spring 2005, Volume 4, Issue 2.

Chapters

"An Anthropologist's Reflections on the Writings of Monica Wilson." In *Confronting Social Change in Africa: Reflections of the Life, Work and Legacy of Monica Hunter Wilson*. Edited by Lesley Banks and Andrew Banks (forthcoming).

"Mapping the Conflict." In *anthropologies*. Edited by Richard Baxstrom and Todd Meyers. Creative Capitalism, 2008.

"Neutralizing the Young: The South African Truth and Reconciliation Commission and Youth." In *On Knowing and Not*

Knowing in the Anthropology of Medicine. Edited by Roland Littlewood. Left Coast Press, 2007.

"Afterword." In *Under Fire: Childhood in the Shadow of War.* Edited by Andrea Immel and Elizabeth Goodenough. Wayne State University Press, 2007.

"Forming Identities: Conceptions of Pain and Children's Expressions of Pain in South Africa." In *Makers and Breakers, Made and Broken: Children and Youth as Emerging Categories in Postcolonial Africa.* Edited by Alcinda Honwana and Filip de Boeck. Oxford: James Currey Publishers, 2005.

"Adolescents and Individuality." In *The Tonga-Speaking Peoples of Zambia and Zimbabwe: Essays in Honor of Elizabeth Colson.* Edited by Ken Vickery. University of America Publishers, 2005.

"Voices not Heard: Small Histories and the Work of Repair" (with Fiona C. Ross). In *To Repair the Irreparable: Reparations and Reconstruction in South Africa.* Edited by Erik Doxtader and Charles Villa-Vicencio. The Institute for Justice and Reconciliation, 2004.

"Youth, War and Contested Childhoods. An Introductory Essay." In *Youth Activism: An International Encyclopaedia.* Edited by Lonnie Sherrod and Connie Flanagan. Greenwood Press, 2005.

"Adolescents and Individuality." In *The Tonga-Speaking Peoples of Zambia and Zimbabwe: Essays in Honor of Elizabeth Colson.* Edited by Ken Vickery. University of America Publishers, 2005.

"'Where Wings Take Dream' On Children in the Work of War and the War of Work." In *Children and Youth on the Frontline: Ethnography, Armed Conflict and Displacement.* Edited by Jo Boyden and Jo de Berry. Berghahn Books, 2005. (First Published in *The Journal of the International Institute*, Winter 2002, Volume 9, Issue 2).

"The Ground of All Making: State Violence, the Family and Political Activists." In *Violence and Subjectivity.* Edited by Veena Das, Arthur Kleinman, Pamela Reynolds, and Mamphela Ramphele. University of California Press, 2000.

"Activism, Politics and the Punishment of Children." In *Childhood Abused.* Edited by Geraldine Van Bueren. Aldershot, Ashgate Publishers, 1998.

"Vision: Well Being and Suffering." In *Mental Health Policy Issues for South Africa.* Edited by D. Foster, M. Freeman and Y. Pillay. Cape Town, MASA Multimedia, 1997.

"Youth and the Politics of Culture in South Africa." In *Children and the Politics of Culture.* Edited by Sharon Stephens. Princeton University Press, 1995.

"Dreams and the Constitution of Self Among the Zezuru." In *Dreaming, Religion and Society.* Edited by M.C. Jedrej and R. Shaw. Leiden, E.J. Brill, 1990.

"Through the Looking Glass: Participant Observation with Children in southern Africa." In *Through the Looking Glass: Children and Health Promotion.* Edited by J. Ross and V. Bergum. Canadian Public Health Association, 1990.

"Healing Children's Trauma after War." In *Children on the Front Line. The Impact of Apartheid, Destabilisation and Warfare on Children in Southern and South Africa.* A Report for UNICEF, United Nations Children's Fund, 1989 (Third Edition).

"The Training of Traditional Healers in Mashonaland." In *The Professionalisation of African Medicine.* Edited by Murray Last and Gordon L Chavunduka. Manchester University Press, 1986.

"Men without Children." *Second Carnegie Inquiry into Poverty and Development in Southern Africa,* Conference Paper No. 5, SALDRU, University of Cape Town, 1984.

Articles

"Imfobe: Self-knowledge and the Reach for Ethics among Former, Young, Anti-Apartheid Activists." *Anthropology Southern Africa Journal* 2005, 28 (3 and 4): 62-72.

"'Not Known Because Not Looked For': Ethnographers Listening to the Young in Southern Africa." *Ethnos. Journal of the National Museum of Ethnography,* Stockholm, 1995, 60 (3-4): 193-221.

"Wrapped in Pain: Moral Economies and the South African TRC." (with Fiona Ross) *Context* 1999, 3 (1): 1-9.

"Zezuru Turn of the Screw. On Children's Exposure to Evil." *Culture, Medicine and Psychiatry* 1990, 14 (3): 313-337.

"Children of Tribulation: The Need to Heal and the Means to Heal War Trauma." *Africa* 1990, 60 (1): 1-38.

"The Double Strategy of Children in South Africa." *Sociological Studies of Child Development* 1989, 1 (3): 113-137.

"Concepts of Childhood Drawn from the Ideas and Practice of Traditional Healers in Musami." *Zambezia* 1986, 13 (1): 1-10.

"Children in Zimbabwe. Rights and Power in Relation to Work." *Anthropology Today* 1985, 1 (3): 16-20.

Contributors

Thomas Cousins is Clarendon-Lienhardt Associate Professor in the Social Anthropology of Africa, Oxford University.

Stefanos Geroulanos is Associate Professor of History at New York University.

Todd Meyers is Associate Professor of Anthropology and Director of the Center for Society, Health, and Medicine at New York University–Shanghai.

Fiona C. Ross is Professor and Head of Anthropology, School of African and Gender Studies, Anthropology, and Linguistics, University of Cape Town.

Vaibhav Saria is Postdoctoral Research Fellow at Institute of Socio-Economic Research on Development and Democracy (ISERDD).

Printed in the United States
By Bookmasters